WHEN IN ROME

SUNY Series in Philosophy
Robert C. Neville, Editor

When in Rome

AN INTRODUCTION TO RELATIVISM AND KNOWLEDGE

N. L. Gifford

State University of New York Press
ALBANY

Published by State University of New York Press, Albany
Printed in the United States of America

For information, address State University of New York Press, State University Plaza, Albany, N.Y., 12246

Library of Congress Cataloging in Publication Data

Gifford, N. L. 1946–
When in Rome.

(SUNY series in philosophy)
Includes index.
1. Relativism. 2. Knowledge, Theory of.
I. Title. II. Series.
BD221.G53   1983   121   82-10374
ISBN 0-87395-667-2
ISBN 0-87395-668-0 (pbk.)

To
Alice M. Gifford,
with love and thanks

Contents

Preface

"Whether or not God exists for me, He can exist for you."

"Whether or not taking bribes is dishonest just depends on how you define 'honesty'."

"A college degree is important only because our society says it is."

These statements represent relativism in saying that whatever we know will primarily depend on—be relative to—either something about a person (e.g., whether you believe that God exists), or something distinctive in the context (e.g., how we will define "honesty" in this particular situation), or the beliefs of our culture (e.g., a college degree might be thought worthless in another culture).

Normally we do not expect knowledge to be so personal or variable. We think that when we *know* something about the world, what we know is both true and obvious to others as well. The focus of *When in Rome* is on what we can know, i.e., when we can confidently describe something about the world and be assured that we are right. As I watch the bird out my window and ask you to listen to its song, I don't worry about whether you will believe there is a bird there or how we are to define "song." I assume we see the same thing, hear the same thing and will claim to know the same thing, namely that there is a singing bird outside the window.

Any inquiry into knowledge will attempt to uncover a standard or criterion that we can use to show that what we say is right. Having such a standard can offer this confidence and assurance that we can know the world. The relativist, on the other hand, will deny that we can ever offer a single criterion by which we can determine the "rightness" of what we claim. Rather, says the relativist, what we know will vary with the unique features of a person or of a context or of a culture, as in the examples listed above.

When the nonrelativist says that knowledge will not vary from person to person, situation to situation or culture to culture, this means that there are things and events in the world which exist independently. In the above examples, the nonrelativist would seek to show that God exists independently of what you or I believe, that taking bribes is wrong in every situation, that education benefits a student regardless of the value placed on it by another culture. Our knowledge of these claims, then, will not vary with our personal beliefs or the beliefs of our culture.

Even if we don't consider ourselves relativists, the position is popularized in the clichés of our language: "When in Rome, do as the Romans do" (meaning that what one should do in a particular place is relative to the customs of that place), "Beauty is in the eye of the beholder" (meaning that standards of excellence are relative to personal likes and dislikes), or "The end justifies the means" (meaning that the integrity of what you do is relative to what you ultimately achieve). In one way or another we are affected by the position I am calling "popular relativism" (the form of relativism that appears in our ordinary, everyday conversations). Hence, you may want to understand what that position is and how it may affect us, whether or not you agree with it.

Often your first acquaintance with popular relativism is in casual conversations about what you should do or about things you like. You might say (or hear) "There is no right or wrong, only how you feel about something" when discussing what you should do, or "It all comes down to what you like" when debating whether a concert was any good. The approach taken by *When in Rome* is to place these conclusions within a broader perspective of how these answers entail a particular view of knowledge and how they can affect how we see the world and act in the world. Rather than seeing relativism in only its ethical dimension or aesthetic dimension, I am suggesting that putting the response of relativism in the context of problems of knowledge offers a sound framework within which to understand the claims made by ethical or aesthetic relativists. But, you may reply, at least I know something about what I think I should do and what I like. What do I know about problems of knowledge?

Problems of knowledge arise from our own experiences that we cannot explain. Philosophers are simply those people who—along with natural and social scientists—have taken on the task of trying to explain puzzling aspects of our familiar world. If you've ever briefly wondered how reliable your perception really is (say the first time you saw water on the road ahead and slowed down only to reach dry pavement, or felt sure you heard a friend's car pull up, only to find no car had pulled up at all), you've encountered one of these puzzles.

If you've ever thought about the difference between your own private experiences of hopes and dreams and disappointments and feelings and the more "public" world around you where people attend class, teach class, write papers, go to parties, you've begun exploring the difficult relationship between how your private experiences can bring you to know the public world. If you've felt uneasy with seemingly radical changes in your life (e.g., estrangement from a valued friend, a run of bad luck), you might find yourself questioning what you thought you knew.

If you've ever thought about what kind of life you would be leading in another culture, or what kind of person you would be or whether you would be any different at all raised in another time or another place, you've begun to deal with the puzzle of what really makes up your own identity and how you are able to "know yourself." In one way or another, relativism seems to offer some very appealing and often interesting responses to these various concerns.

In addition to introducing us to these problems of knowledge, the discussion of popular relativism may introduce us as well to our own conflicting beliefs about knowledge. The conflict appears in the frequent use we make of relativism ("Whatever's right for you") while at the same time we may want or expect there to be an objective standard which enables us to prove that what we're saying is right ("If you would only take a look at the unemployment figures, you would see this is not a good time to quit your job."). It's not helpful to say we can be relativists about some things but not about others, in response to this conflict. If we do say this, we are in effect volunteering to give up the assurance and guarantee we want from knowledge. At the very least, *When in Rome* can acquaint you with your own expectations for knowledge and enable you to decide for yourself what you may or may not want to give up.

As we will see in the text, relativism competes with other, nonrelativistic approaches to the questions and concerns we have about our world. Since these questions are so important, the differences between the competing positions should be carefully considered. Whether we adopt relativism or reject it will make quite a difference as to how we see ourselves, how we experience the world, and how we behave. *When in Rome* takes the stance that popular relativism cannot adequately "solve" the problems of knowledge mentioned above. However, relativism does make a vital and valuable contribution to our understanding of these problems.

By taking a position on issues and concerns in the world, relativism is able to introduce us to many of these issues, particularly if we aren't accustomed to joining debates about them. Taking a position on something—"Abortion is justified," or "Reagan should be more careful about cutting assistance"—may seem to some of you natural and all in a day's conversation. However, taking a position on an issue requires more independence of thought (i.e., knowing what *you* think or feel about something) than we may be equipped for. Our education, in stressing the accumulation of a vast quantity of facts and information, may slight the skills and confidence needed to "take a stand" and argue in favor of or against a position.

In other words, our classroom experiences may not have included much attention to helping us formulate our own thoughts or to conveying them clearly, to evaluating and justifying what we think. But without practice in developing these skills and without the confidence to say what we think, we cannot become independent thinkers. We may even withdraw from debate or dialogue feeling inadequate, tongue-tied and very anxious. Because it is an issue-oriented approach, an examination of relativism can offer you a means of beginning to sort out your own thoughts about the world and what you can know about the world. It can also give you a way of participating in the many important debates about issues in our world.

Hence, popular relativism needs to be carefully and sympathetically presented and discussed. Unfortunately this is not always possible in the classroom. Even in my own classes in philosophy, there is often too little time to pursue lengthy discussions of what relativism is and what it can or can't do. Because of this concern with time, it may appear to you as if your interest in relativism is thought trivial or unimportant. That is far from the case, as I suggest in this book. Your response to a problem suggests that not only do you understand what's going on but you have made these concerns your own. I mean by this that you are not just sitting around memorizing what some philosopher says but you have begun to see that the problem affects you and your world, and you have as much at stake in the outcome as does the philosopher. Also, you are asserting your right to participate in the solution as well as claim a place for yourself in the arena of intellectual debate.

The text of *When in Rome*, then, will combine discussion of popular relativism with discussion of some philosophical problems of knowledge (to the extent that these problems can help us to better understand relativism). Chapter One introduces our standard conception of knowledge, the con-

ception we use most often (though may not be aware of) in
our normal, daily transactions in the world. Chapter Two
opens the discussion of relativism with the obvious starting
point of what we know about ourselves and how we see
the world or personally feel about issues in the world. This
discussion of "subjective knowledge" (to be found in Sections
6 and 8) introduces the position of Naive Relativism, loosely
the form of relativism which says that if I think something
is true, then it *is* true [for me].

Chapter Three, Sections 10, 11 and 14, moves to a broader
view of what we can know about the world, by considering
the context of the various situations in which we often find
ourselves. Here we are introduced to Context Relativism, the
position which says that knowledge and action depend on
special features of a particular situation; for example, you
may rationalize not going to class today on the grounds that
you are too tired right now and have other things to do (but
you'll go next time).

Chapter Four, Sections 16, 17 and 20, takes the broadest
and most comprehensive view of what we can know about
the world. The Cultural Relativist in that chapter will want
to say that whatever we know and do depends on our
cultural beliefs, values and practices. For example, in our
society it is important to know how to drive a car and open
a checking account, but this would be totally irrelevant to
a person living on our continent during the twelfth century.
In Chapter Five, Section 23 reviews these three versions of
popular relativism and takes up some of the questions not
yet dealt with.

The remaining sections of the book try to acquaint you
informally with what philosophers do as well as to engage
you in some philosophical inquiry. It sounds formidable, but
the *activity* of doing philosophy is familiar to all of us (e.g.,
seeking reasons, and evaluating them, for what we think
and do). What might appear difficult is the way in which
philosophers conduct their work, the way questions are posed
and investigated, the technical jargon needed to carry on
precise investigation. As with any encounter with something
new, you might well feel awkward, out of your element and

often confused—as if some important point must have flown by while you were looking the other way.

On the other hand, there are some appealing benefits to taking on this new mode of inquiry. You have the chance to consider puzzling features of your experiences in a new light. You can put yourself in a position to *choose* what you believe and what you want to do. You may come to understand past choices. You might find a way to resolve current confusions. To these ends, I hope that *When in Rome* can prove useful.

Acknowledgments

I am deeply grateful to my family, friends and colleagues for their help and for the faith they have had in *When in Rome*. It has grown and flourished under their care and attention.

I would like to thank Dr. Susan Wood for her initial support, encouragement and help in writing "The Uses and Abuses of Relativism," the paper from which this book grew.

I would also like to thank Niall Caldwell for his sustained involvement and contribution to *When in Rome*. This means two years of discussion and debate, prodding and encouragement, patience and quick response to the often outrageous demands made of him.

Special notes of thanks are due each of the persons who have shared their time and interest. In particular I would like to thank Ted Bohn, Drs. David Pomerantz, Patrick Heelan and Helen Heise, and Kathi Hayes for their generosity, quick wits and unceasing efforts on behalf of the book.

Already it is easy to see that many talented people participated in the emergence of *When in Rome*. Including those mentioned, I am deeply grateful to those who put their own concerns aside to patiently and enthusiastically respond to a problem I would thrust upon them. These kind people include Laurie Lewis, Tod Mijanovich, Drs. Marjorie Miller, Patrick

Grim, and Donn Welton, Patrice Yourdon, Will Reynolds, Michael Brown, Bob Crosby, Ann Millikin and Dr. Robert Swartz. To each I offer my thanks, with some chagrin for appropriating their time as if it were my own.

I was also inspired and gratified by the thoughtful reading and helpful comments given to *When in Rome*. My thanks for this go to Drs. Joyce Henricks, Marshall Spector, Patrick Hill, David Hicks, Nancy Cartwright, Ernest Sosa, Richard Schmitt, Eric Goode, Brett Silverstein, and Harvey Farberman, as well as to Elizabeth Lazeski, Michael Miller, Jim Whitcomb and George Messier.

I am grateful to the Board of Control of the John Anson Kittredge Educational Fund, John F. Kennedy School of Government at Harvard University, for their financial support of the research which made *When in Rome* possible. I would like, particularly, to thank Ernest R. May, Chairman of the Kittredge Educational Fund, for his advice and help.

A special thanks goes to Dr. Robert Neville for his encouragement, and to William Eastman of SUNY Press for his faith in *When in Rome*. I would also like to thank the members of the Philosophy Department of SUNY/Stony Brook, particularly Mary Bruno and Terry Hogan, for their generosity; most of the text was composed in the supportive environment of that department. A very special thanks, finally, goes to Catherine and Eddie Coady.

Each of these people has helped *When in Rome* become the book I envisioned and I can only begin to thank them here.

N.L.G.
University of Massachusetts/Boston
April 1982

CHAPTER ONE
The Problem of Knowledge

1. Knowledge, Who Needs It?

I pull out my keys, open the door to my office, go inside and drop my book bag on the nearest chair. You come home, put a record on the turntable and listen to a familiar tune while you go to the refrigerator. Both events are normal and predictable in our daily life. The actions may be so habitual that we can easily do them while we are preoccupied with other thoughts.

Though we don't have to think about what we are doing, we use a rather considerable amount of knowledge to be able to do these mundane tasks. For example, to enter my office I must know that there is a door here, that I have a key to open it, that this is the right key, that the door opens into my office, that this *is* my office, that this is a chair, that the chair will support my book bag. Similarly, you depend on knowing that you are home, that this is a record, that this record will play songs by the artist listed on the cover, that this is a turntable, that you can activate the turntable in this way, that you are hearing what you expected to hear, that this is a refrigerator.

Though we may both agree that we must know these things, you might well point out to me that we hardly need

1

to list these things in order to get the record on and something to eat from the refrigerator. We don't even need to think about what we know to continue our daily tasks; we are just able to do what we set out to do. Isn't that enough?

It might well be. At least it would be if our lives were solely constituted by repetitious actions, if we weren't ever curious, if we didn't want to evaluate what we are doing or how we are doing. That is, if our life were wholly predictable and if we were wholly satisfied with it, perhaps we wouldn't think to ask what we know or how we know it.

But we are often unable to do what we expect to do. Or something happens to us that we don't understand. In one way or another, our world is temporarily disrupted. Very often we respond with curiosity, seeking both to understand what has happened and to restore order. If you arrive home to find your turntable gone, you would not continue on to the refrigerator. Most likely you would immediately seek some sort of explanation. Are other things missing? Disturbed? Did you promise to loan the turntable to a friend? Would anyone you know just come in and take it? Did you forget that you took it to the repair shop?

In this brief look at some trivial actions of our lives, we can begin to see emerging the role that knowledge plays. Such a role might be characterized as: (a) providing a basis for predictable action, (b) explaining what we seek to understand, (c) providing a direction for investigation to satisfy our curiosity, and (d) enabling us to control a greater portion of our lives.

In order for knowledge to realize fully such a role, we need to make sure that our concept of knowledge is adequate. I mean by this that whatever we know should be able to fulfill this role in our lives. In other words, how we account for knowing will affect the extent to which we can utilize the above role of knowledge. If, in 1492, we claim to "know" the world is flat on the grounds that everybody "knows" it, we won't be able to explain why Columbus didn't fall off the edge on his sea voyage nor can we predict where he will end up as he embarks on his voyage. Appealing to "everyone knows it" keeps me from asking further questions or seeking a better explanation; we are satisfied that we know.

Many of our beliefs are neither useful nor justified, though we feel satisfied that we "know" much about the world on the basis of these beliefs. We accept many of the beliefs of our family, our friends, educators, and the media. We develop our own beliefs from our various experiences in the world. This is hardly a systematic set of beliefs; most are acquired casually, even accidentally, often uncritically or with little awareness that we are taking on new beliefs.

We will be limited, however, much as Columbus was, in what we can accomplish and conceive for ourselves, unless we are able to distinguish systematically between reliable and unreliable beliefs. One way to distinguish between beliefs is to formulate a criterion which we can apply to every belief we hold to see which ones can legitimately count as knowledge. Such a criterion will list all the conditions which must be satisfied before we can say we know something.

The concept of knowledge as true, justified belief does provide such a list. Before I can claim I know something, my belief must be shown to be both true and justified. In this way I can keep from making the mistake of taking prejudice or opinion as knowledge. If you reflect upon your own conversations with others, you may see that you yourself have actually appealed to this concept of knowledge. Perhaps you dismissed a friend's belief on the grounds that s/he couldn't prove it and you have evidence that the belief is false. In effect, you are saying that a belief must be both true and justified before it can be accepted as knowledge.

This concept of knowledge as true, justified belief is the standard view of knowledge. I call it the "standard view" because it is the concept most prevalent in our normal, everyday way of investigating the world. It is also the view found in our intellectual history, i.e., Western thought has continually supported the view that knowledge is true, justified belief, though there have been many debates and disagreements about this. Since you might be wondering why you've never heard about this standard view, it is because we normally use it and rarely discuss it; this chapter will review what this concept of knowledge is.

The first thing to notice is that we make a distinction between "belief" and "knowledge." To say that I believe there is a door here or that you believe you are home seems far too weak. You would *know* whether or not you are home. We usually speak in terms of "belief" when there is a chance that we might be wrong. "I believe the turntable is in the living room unless my roommate took it to the repair shop for me," you might say.

If, in fact, the turntable is in the living room, your belief will be true. However, since you are not sure that it's there, you would not claim to know it's there, even though it is. This, of course, does *not* mean that feeling quite sure is enough to claim knowledge. You may feel quite sure that you passed the test without studying when in fact you have failed. When feeling sure arises from knowing that your evidence is sound and complete, then the feeling has some basis. You can, if need be, produce the evidence which supports your knowledge claim. By itself, however, feeling sure is no indication of knowledge.

Let's say that a burglar did not take your stereo nor did your roommate take it to the repair shop. Let's say that you took it to the repair shop yourself. If you recalled the sequence of events—packing it up that morning, putting it in the car, driving to the repair shop, dropping it off—you would expect your turntable to be gone. The chain of evidence leaves no doubt in your mind that the turntable is at the repair shop and not in the living room of your home. Your *belief*, in this case, is both *true* (because the turntable is at the repair shop) and *justified* (you can cite the specific events involved in getting it to the shop).

It seems reasonable, then, to analyze knowledge as true, justified belief. If this is an adequate account of knowledge, we will be able to check our own beliefs and see which ones will count as knowledge. But there is an additional consideration: how do we tell if our evidence is good enough? For example, "I think Jones's house has green shutters" will not get somebody to Jones's house as easily as "Jones live at 232 Forest Lane." Though we can easily see the difference here, we should say what makes this difference.

2. "I'm from Missouri—Show Me"

In effect, the evidence that we appeal to will show our belief to be true (or at least sound). Arriving at truth, then, is a process of justification. Demonstrating the truth of my belief will not depend on how persuasive I am nor will it depend on how loudly I insist that the belief is true. The standard view of knowledge (that knowledge is true, justified belief) usually holds that our justification will be adequate if we can show the belief to be "objective" and "universal." If we can, we are in a position to claim that the belief is true.[1]

To claim your belief is "objective" is simply to claim that what you believe *is* in fact in the world. If you know that your turntable is in your living room, ready to be used, you will expect that it will look much the same to any person observing it: you expect that its particular characteristics will remain constant. Likewise, in directing someone to Jones's house, you claim that there *is* a residence at 232 Forest Lane (in Middletown, New York) and that Jones occupies that residence.

To claim that your belief is "universal" is to say that any normal person in these circumstances will see the turntable (when they enter your living room) and will be able to find Jones's home and discover that he lives there.

If there is any doubt in your mind that you do expect your claims to knowledge to be both universal and objective, listen closely to what you say. It's likely that you will expect

---

1. Here we should distinguish conditions for knowledge from conditions for truth since the text shifts from one to the other. However, to insist on this distinction might well be confusing as you are being introduced to our standard view of knowledge. Intuitively, though, you can well see that showing truth and showing knowledge of a belief may not be identical procedures.

others to "see," or be able to see, the "rightness" of some
of what you say. You expect them to see what you see and
describe objects much as you do: "Well just look on the
table; the felt-tip pen is right on top," you might say in an
exasperated tone.

One answer to our question of what will count as good
enough evidence to be able to claim knowledge might be
when we are able to show our belief to be objective and
universal. Some of our claims in Section 1 are easily checked.
Anyone can tell there is a door here with a lock on it; anyone
can tell, when the door is opened, that this is an office and
that there are several chairs in the office. Similarly, anyone
will be able to identify the turntable if they are in your
living room, select records (even if the artists are unfamiliar),
activate the turntable and see the refrigerator (under normal
circumstances). And these objects will appear essentially the
same to any observer. If you have a new green Frigidare,
the observer will not see a white Hotpoint from the forties,
i.e., the characteristics remain constant even if our observer
can't identify distinct brands.

However, it would be ridiculous to assume that everyone
knows this to be my office or your living room, which key
will open the door or whether I even have a key, and what
a particular song by a particular artist will sound like. Does
this mean, then, that many of our claims to knowledge *can't*
be universal? Each of us seems to know a great many things
that others are unlikely to know: I know what my plans for
the day are, you know the distinctive piano style of Mose
Allison. Similarly you might wonder how objective our claims
to knowledge can be. As we both exit from the same class
I might say, "That was really interesting," whereas you might
be thinking how boring it had been.

Often when we encounter these differences it seems only
reasonable to conclude that perhaps we shouldn't insist upon
a single standard by which to judge what will count as
knowledge. We will sometimes say, "It [knowledge] is really
just a matter of opinion." We may often say this, while at
the same time we still expect others to see what we do and
make the same claims about the world as we do (e.g., seeing

that the felt-tip pen is on top of the table, knowing what time it is). This expectation is the appeal to objectivity and universality in knowledge, that there are (and should be) objective standards and procedures by which to determine what we know.

When we say "Knowledge is just a matter of opinion," we are recommending that we give up objectivity and universality as a means of showing the adequacy of our evidence. Since our inquiry into knowledge is just beginning, we are faced with a choice of how to conduct this inquiry: we can continue with the strategy of showing the objectivity and universality in *all* claims to knowledge, or we can reject this strategy in favor of showing the irreconcilable differences and variations in the things we claim to know.

I, as the author, will opt for the first choice, but not on the grounds that it is right or necessary, for I have not yet demonstrated the rightness or necessity of keeping objectivity and universality in knowledge. The grounds on which I make this choice reflects, for the most part, my preferences. I would rather knowledge be objective and universal. If it is, I will be assured of living in a "public" world, the same world that others live in and perceive; my communication with others in the world will refer to the same world. In other words, my interactions with a public world will be more successful and predictable if, in fact, I am able to show that knowledge is objective and universal.

Notice that my decision to pursue the first course of action is represented in terms of what seems most reasonable as well as my preferences for the eventual outcome. Notice that I am not assuming the truth of what I am seeking to show, but in order to proceed I will act as if it is true. In other words, I make a tentative commitment to a particular course of investigation.

If I were to reject the possibility of objectivity and universality immediately, I would pursue a different course of investigation. I would tentatively be committed to the position that knowledge claims will manifest different characteristics: i.e., that "This is my office" is different from "Here is a chair," for not everyone can say "This is my office." I might proceed by listing the different kinds of knowledge claims, or I might assume knowledge claims can't be classified.

However, the need here (given my choice of how to pursue the inquiry) is to show objectivity and universality in knowledge. This means I will take on the task of untangling the apparent differences in our knowledge claims. Ultimately, I will try to show how objectivity and universality are possible even for biographical claims such as "This is my office." Whether or not my choice is vindicated will be determined when I offer the results of my investigation so that you can compare them with the results offered by the position denying the possibility of objectivity and universality.

3. Have a Seat

At this point, we should return to our familiar world of objects and events to see what in fact we are talking about in these claims to knowledge. There is a rather broad range of things we seem to know and need to know about our world. I am referring primarily to the physical world. Adopting the terminology of philosophers, I will often use the word "empirical" when I am referring to the world we live in. "Empirical," though, refers to more than chairs and turntables; it may include, as well, abstract features of the physical world such as ideas and relationships. For example, our concept of education is not tangible in the way a chair is, but is part of our world nonetheless. When we say "All citizens have a right to be educated" we are talking about our attitude toward education. But it's more than an attitude, for admission policies of universities will be affected, colleges will be designed to accomodate large numbers of students, and faculty will be expected to address an audience of diverse backgrounds and skills.

The range of empirical belief will include particular statements such as "Here is a chair" or "There is a turntable." Empirical belief will also include general claims such as

"Water freezes at 32° Fahrenheit" as well as adages and metaphors of our culture: "A stitch in time saves nine."[2]

These examples are fairly straightforward (unlike our original list which included statements that perhaps only you or I would know). "Objective" as a property of a statement, as we have seen in the preceding section, means that the statement accurately depicts or represents something that really is in the world. The literal meaning of "objective" is "of an object" (as distinct from a person or "subject"). An object is something clearly separate from us, most obviously things like turntables, chairs, trees and dogs, less obviously things like our educational practices and ideas about how to raise children. The above claims represent, respectively, that there is a chair before me or there is a turntable before you, that [pure] water does freeze at 32° Fahrenheit, that one can avoid unnecessary labor if one takes the time to complete a task (and, if we include ethical statements, that killing is wrong).

"Universality" means that anyone in these circumstances would make the same claim. Surely, any person standing where I am now standing will see the chair, just as any person standing where you are in your living room will see the turntable. (Hence, our claims are not figments of our imaginations.) Any person investigating the dispositional properties of water will find that [pure] water freezes at 32° Fahrenheit. Any person can save time and labor by fully completing a task. (If we include ethical claims, we would say that any person reflecting on the morality of killing would conclude that killing is wrong.)

Notice that we can easily identify the objectivity and universality of *these* statements, whereas there were some not so easily recognized as objective and universal in our

---

2. Some philosophers would also include ethical statements such as "Thou shalt not kill" in our body of empirical knowledge. To do this they will have to show these claims to be objective and universal. There are many fuzzy areas in addition to ethics as well. However, the point here is just to get an idea of what empirical belief is.

original list. (Even though anyone might see this office as an office, they would not necessarily know it to be *my* office.) The difference is that here we can determine whether or not the statement is true by looking at something in the world. What will make the claim true or false is whether or not there really *is* a chair here and whether anyone *could* in fact claim that there is a chair here. The truth or falsity of the statement does *not* depend on whether I've had my eyes checked or whether I'm preoccupied or whether I even know what a chair is. There is an object here, having distinctive characteristics, and even if I were the most naive of observers I would still be presented with the same characteristics that appear to a more sophisticated observer.

This view is based on saying that the *truth conditions* for this statement are given solely by reference to what is in the "public" world. The conditions, for example, under which "Here is a chair" will be true, will be the presence of a chair before me. The conditions under which "Water freezes at 32° Fahrenheit" is true, is the freezing of water when the temperature drops to that point or below. That is, what makes these claims true or false is totally independent of who happens to be around, independent of whether anyone is around at all. The claims would still be true. My chair will still be in my office after I leave, water will continue to freeze in remote wilderness areas.

But some of the statements in the original list in Section 1 seem to depend upon the presence of a particular person in order to be true. I can say "This is my office" but you can't. You can say "I am in my living room" but I can't even if I am standing where you are. Similarly, I can't say "This is my office" if I am driving home. The *truth conditions* of these statements seem to require reference to where *I* am as well as to *who* I am. So even though "my" office is part of the public world, just as "your" living room and turntable are, showing the objectivity and universality of these statements is not so straightforward as showing the objectivity and universality of the empirical beliefs discussed in this section.

What is important at this point is to understand that we will be discussing the knowledge that we can have about the "public" world: that we are talking about objects, events, people and places that we encounter daily; the things we recognize as part of our world and which are, for the most part, thoroughly familiar to us. This is the world that is known.

For our beliefs about this world to count as knowledge, the beliefs must be true and justified.[3] One way to show that we have true, justified belief is to show that the belief is objective and universal. As we have seen, this means showing that the truth conditions for each belief are given by reference to the objects, events and places in the public world, rather than by reference to our own moods or opinions. If we can show this, then the world around us can truly be said to be known.

4. Belief, Everybody's Got One

Even if truth conditions are given solely by reference to "external" things and events, *we* are still very much a part of an adequate account of knowledge. Whereas "truth" and "evidence" might be demonstrable by appeal to the public world, "belief" is always a belief held by a particular person. *I* believe that it will not snow today and *you* believe that the library closes at 10 P.M. The library certainly doesn't believe anything nor do the blue skies above.

The fact that belief is part of our account of knowledge is neither surprising nor unreasonable. There are, however, two separate points involved that we will need to discuss.

---

3. There is current debate about whether these three conditions—belief, truth, justification—are sufficient for knowledge; the suggestion is that there should be a fourth condition. The need for this fourth condition was presented by E. Gettier in "Is Justified True Belief Knowledge?" in *Analysis* 23 (1963), 121–23 and discussed by K. Lehrer and T. Paxson (among others) in "Knowledge: Undefeated Justified True Belief" in *Journal of Philosophy* 66, no. 8 (1969), 225–37.

The first is that my believing that it will not snow certainly does not affect the meteorological conditions which will determine whether or not it will snow; nonetheless I would have to believe it will snow if I were to claim that I know that it will snow. The second point is that belief is considered to be a mental activity or state of a particular person. We need to discuss what this means and why we would bring it into our discussion of knowledge when we are trying to show objectivity and universality.

Belief as a mental activity or state of mind may sound like a peculiar way to describe something. However, all of us recognize that each person has "private" states that can't be "seen" or known by others directly. "He must believe the bus will come since he has been standing at the bus stop for an hour." "Ouch, that must hurt," you might say when a person nearby stubs her toe. "I don't know whether he intends to vote for Carter or not." In all three instances, we acknowledge that the other person has a private experience, sensation or belief that we are not having. In the first example, we infer that the gentleman believes the bus will come (perhaps he doesn't know that there is a transit strike). But we don't "see" his belief; we infer such a belief from his actions. In the second case, we empathize with others when they stub their toes, having found that to be quite painful ourselves. We don't feel the pain, but expect that they do. In the third example, we recognize that people have preferences, opinions, intentions that we will not know about unless they tell us about them.

We very normally separate the public world of tables and chairs, trees and dogs, from what we might call the private world of beliefs, desires, physical sensations, hopes, dreams, expectations. This latter world is private simply because each person "knows" his or her own beliefs and desires in a way that no other person can. If I come over to your house to listen to a record, both of us can know the turntable *in the same way*: we can each list the characteristics of the turntable and our lists will match. I, however, cannot know by looking at the turntable or by looking at you what it means to you or how proud you are of having saved to get just the turntable you wanted. This is a natural distinction for us to make everyday. Given the "private" nature of belief, you might now understand why the philosopher wants to insist then on objectivity and universality to show knowledge. Otherwise, we might be saddled with a body of knowledge so variable and idiosyncratic that we might never get anything done.

But why, you might ask, bring in belief at all? If we want knowledge of the public world and belief is really part of a private world, why not just forget belief and talk about what we see before us? This brings us to the first point mentioned above, namely, that belief doesn't affect what really is in the world, but is necessary for claiming to know what is in the world. I think three reasons will explain why we want belief to be a part of knowledge.

(1) The information we get from the external world about what is before us seems to come to us privately. For example, I feel a sensation of pressure against the back of my leg and turn around to see what is there. I see a chair and since I will be here for awhile, I think I'll be seated. The pressure on my leg and my seeing the chair are private and provide enough information for me to seat myself.

(2) When I claim to know something, I am at the same time saying that I am *aware of* this or that object, I am *conscious of* being in this or that situation. It would be odd to suggest that I can say the chair is behind me but I am not aware of it or conscious that it is behind me.

(3) Since we want to be able to provide evidence or justification for our belief (to demonstrate knowledge), we need belief as some sort of intermediary to claiming knowledge. In other words, we want to formulate a tentative commitment, and gather evidence, before we assert knowledge. When we can't gather enough evidence, we can remain tentative: "I believe it will snow today, though I'm not in a position to know."

Belief, then, will be necessary to our account of knowledge. Though what we believe may refer to things in the public world, my belief itself is private, nonuniversal and subjective. Knowing these things about belief also shows us why the philosopher will look for beliefs which are true and justified before claiming knowledge. And, as we have seen, one way to determine whether or not a belief is true is to see if what we believe about the world is objective and universal.

5. The Foundations of Knowledge

If we are going to analyze knowledge as true, justified belief, we are going to want our justification to be reliable and sound. In addition to demonstrating the objectivity and universality of our belief, good evidence should itself be true. That is, the statements we use to justify our empirical belief should be known as well. We would not want to say "I know it's 44° outside" when the thermometer you looked at was, in fact, broken. Even if it is 44° outside, the evidence which you use to claim knowledge is false: the broken thermometer happens to be stuck on 44°. Since it is inoperative, the statement "The thermometer registers 44°" is false; the thermometer only appears to be reporting the temperature but actually isn't.

Two questions might occur to you at this point. Can the statements we use as evidence truly be known themselves? And, relatedly, won't we have to justify our evidential statements (in case they might be false), ending up with an infinite regress of justification (justifying our justification, *ad infinitum*)? Since we cannot be mistaken about the sensations we have (or other states we experience) and these sensations do inform us of the objects in the world around us, we might want to use these "private" states as ultimate justification for our belief. I might appeal to the feeling of resistance against my seat as I sit in the chair. I might report the form and shape I see when I stand up, turn around and take a look at what I was sitting on. I might cite the belief I have that objects having this form and serving the function of seating people are chairs. If I appeal to these "private" states, I cannot be mistaken. Surely I would know and can report accurately the sensation in my seat, nor could I doubt what I see or believe (in the sense that I *do* see this shape and *do* believe that such a shape is a chair). If our justification stops here, with these "private" reports of what we see, feel or believe, we can avoid an infinite regress of justification. ("How do you know your seat feels resistence?" "Because it does." No further proof can be shown.) Also, these reports of what I see, feel or believe are statements that can be known with certainty (since you must know what you feel or believe).

Much of what I do know about the world comes to me through "private" experience, sensation and belief. Of course, this may constitute something of a problem when we need to show objectivity and universality. What I am appealing to here is something about me, not about the world, and something that others will not be likely to see. However, since I cannot be mistaken about my sensations and beliefs, it might provide a valuable *starting point* in constructing a chain of evidence to prove that there is, in fact, a chair here.

Let's say some rampant skeptic challenges your claim that the turntable is in your living room. This may be a reasonable challenge if the skeptic is your roommate who has taken the turntable to the repair shop for you. But if you are both in the living room, either one of you is able to go over to the turntable. You can see it on the shelf, you can select a record, feel the ridged surface of the platter on the turntable, feel the switch as you activate the turntable, see the platter rotate, the record drop and hear what you have chosen. You can send the skeptic to the turntable to get the same information. In the face of such evidence, the challenge can't be reasonably maintained.

The reason this evidence is thought to be so good, as I said above, is that it's hard to imagine how we could be mistaken about our own sensations and private states. If I feel something against the back of my leg, I feel it. If I hope that it will snow, that is something I hope for. The question of justification doesn't arise. Feeling the switch in your hand as you activate the turntable is not something you could be mistaken about or reasonably question (under normal circumstances).

We won't, however, appeal solely to the sensation of feeling the turntable switch. If we did we could only cite something like feeling resistance against our fingers when our hand is in a particular place, which is not very helpful. When the switch is being activated, we feel the sensation of our fingers grasping and turning something, *and we believe* that this particular sensation indicates having the turntable switch in hand. The platter begins rotating, the record drops, the arm swings over, lowers onto the record and we hear the music. We could see the success of our action as further indication that our sensations and beliefs about such sensations correctly indicate what is before us in the public world (even though the sensations and beliefs about these sensations are private).

Since we cannot be mistaken about the private states and experiences we have and since they most often result in successful action, many philosophers will say that we have arrived at the *foundations* of empirical knowledge. This will be the place where our empirical beliefs will be ultimately justified. Also, if we are truly at the foundations of knowledge, we should need no further justification. And, as we have seen, we can't justify any further the fact that I feel my fingers around something. I just do. The fact that the justification "naturally" stops at this point (rather than progressing through more complex lines of reasoning) allows us to show our chain of evidence fairly easily; but most importantly it allows us to show a complete chain of evidence.

With these foundations, I will be able to construct quite a solid chain of evidence to support my belief that the turntable is before me. I can appeal to the various sensations I have, what they seem to indicate about the world, the success of my action. I can send you to the turntable to verify the correctness of my belief. Neither of us can be mistaken about our own states. Both of us can construct an inviolable chain of evidence leading to the same belief that there is a turntable here. And we would expect any other person to be able to do the same under these conditions. So even though the foundations may consist of "subjective" claims, we are able to offer (1) evidence about which we can't be mistaken and (2) a chain of evidence that can be duplicated by *any person* in these circumstances. And we are well on our way to showing universality and objectivity of the belief that there is a turntable here, as well as appropriately claiming knowledge.

Now that we understand how subjective foundations can provide good evidence for objective empirical belief, we can return to the problem that kept cropping up in Sections 2 and 3, namely, that some of our claims to knowledge aren't universal and objective (or don't seem to be). What do we do with these statements? If we are in my office, I can't provide you with a chain of evidence that will allow *you* to say "This is my office."

You might well point out to me that the truth of "This is my office" is relative to the speaker: if I assert the statement and I'm in my office, it will be true; if you assert it, even though you too are in my office, it will be false. And you might well go patiently through the list of remaining "problematic" statements to show me that each is relative in some way to the person who is speaking, where the claim is made, or some other relevant consideration.

We arrive then at the point of debate foreshadowed in the subtitle of the book: An Introduction to Relativism and Knowledge. For as you are patiently showing me how some knowledge claims can't be universal and objective, you are adopting the position of relativism. But since I have already announced (in Section 2) my intention to try to keep universality and objectivity as characteristics of knowledge claims, I will try to change your mind. However, I shall need good reasons to be able to do this, even better than you have for claiming relativism. And, as we will see, relativism can provide a formidable challenge to the traditional conception of knowledge. Which brings us to the need to take a closer look at the various ways knowledge seems to be relative.

CHAPTER TWO
Naive Relativism

6. Beauty Is in the Eye of the Beholder: Subjective Knowledge

In Chapter One we were concerned with objective knowledge, statements describing things and events in the world which anyone could know. This is the conception of knowledge as true, justified belief. In this section and the next, we move to an *opposing* conception of knowledge—that of subjective knowledge. When knowledge is conceived of as subjective we get our first introduction to a full-blown relativist position. In this section, the primary concern is simply to show *what* subjective knowledge is and to show how we can recognize which conception of knowledge we're using.

In the last section, the philosopher suggests that knowledge (objective knowledge) rests on "subjective" foundations. It was pointed out that we can only indirectly know what someone else feels, thinks, believes. That is, we don't have their thoughts or feel their pains, but can infer what they might think or feel. We also saw that much of our ordinary world of tables and chairs is known through sensations. Sensations, like thoughts and pains, are only directly "known" by those having them. You can watch me bump into a chair, but only I will feel the pain in my shin.

18

In one sense it seems that all I can really know is how I see something or feel about something or what I believe:

. . . [E]ach one of us is a measure of what is and of what is not; but there is all the difference in the world between one man and another just in the very fact that what is and appears to one is different from what is and appears to the other.[1]

In this quote, Plato is representing the position of another Greek philosopher, Protagoras. "Each one of us is a measure of what is and of what is not." A measure is a standard or criterion by which we make judgments. Protagoras suggests that what I know about the world depends on what I've seen and how I've seen it. In other words, the judgments I make about the world will come from *my* particular experiences in the world. Each of us has different personal histories, different hopes, different possibilities. (Isn't the world of a rock star quite different from the world of a student?)

The quote "There is all the difference between what appears to one person and what appears to another" (to paraphrase) acknowledges the disagreements we have about what we see. "Whose yellow car is parked in front?" "That's not yellow, it's light green." "You're crazy. It's yellow." "Look again, it's light green." Sometimes, in exasperation we might say "Okay, to me it's light green, to you it's yellow." In effect what we are doing is agreeing with Protagoras and allowing knowledge to be "subjective and relative" rather than objective and universal.

A "subjective" statement will describe a state of a subject or person. States of a person will include, as we have seen, beliefs, desires, hopes, dreams, expectations, feelings, sensations, imaginings, emotions. Such states are thought to be private. Only I can really know if I have a headache; others can only know that I do when I furrow my brow or complain, but they don't feel the pain. In other words, a subjective

---

1. Plato, *Theatetus*, trans. F.M. Cornford (New York: Bobbs-Merrill, n.d.) p. 160.

statement will describe something private about a person, an objective statement will describe something public about the world. (We are not here contrasting abstract notions of subjectivity and objectivity. We are contrasting two different types of statements, different with respect to what they depict or represent, a person or the world.)

Knowledge that is "relative" will consist of statements whose truth depends on the state of a person, beliefs of a particular group or culture, or particular features of the environment. We have, however, only been discussing states of a person here. The position that truth is dependent on the states of a particular person is what I will call "Naive Relativism." The quote above, "Each one of us is the measure of what is and of what is not," is an example of this position. The Naive Relativist will claim that the truth of any statement is relative to the beliefs of a particular person.

In assessing claims to knowledge we sometimes hear Naive Relativism put in the form of "true for me, true for you." For example, even though we would not say that the car could be both green and yellow at the same time, we might say "For you it's green, for me it's yellow," acknowledging that it does appear to me to be green and to you to be yellow.

Often we hear "(For me) school is a waste of time," "You may think that class has something to offer but I don't feel that way," "I just don't see that logic has anything to do with the world." In each case, the presumption is that the truth value is determined by the speaker. Another person might claim exactly the opposite: "School is invaluable," "That class really makes me think," "Logic helps me to argue more effectively." Since the truth value of the sentences are determined by the speaker, the statements will not be seen to be contradictory. Whereas "School is a waste of time and school is invaluable" might be contradictory, "Jones believes that school is a waste of time and Smith believes that school is invaluable" is not thought to be.

In other words, to avoid such a contradiction we may talk about Smith and Jones instead of about school. However, we often intend to say something about school itself, not

about Smith or Jones. And we may present the above statements as claims to knowledge about the world, not as simply
depicting attitudes of Smith or Jones. What is important here
is to recognize this distinction. If we debate the merits of
school and offer good evidence for our positions, we are
following the recommendations of Chapter One and are
accepting the concept of knowledge as true, justified belief.

Such belief is justified by showing it to be objective and
universal. In talking about school itself, our belief is objective:
we are referring to an educational institution, curriculum,
faculty, etc. that exists in the world independently of Smith
and Jones. In expecting that we can successfully defend our
position and that any person will recognize the worth of our
position, we are claiming that our belief is universal: if you
argue that "School is valuable" on the grounds, say, that
school offers systematic training in the critical skills of thinking, reasoning, argumentation and evaluation, you believe
that I (and anyone else) will come to see the value of school.

If, on the other hand, we resolve the debate by appealing
to the attitudes of Smith and Jones, we simply stop talking
about school. Now we are talking about Smith and about
Jones. If we think this is the only means of resolution, we
are saying that knowledge is really subjective (descriptive of
what Smith or Jones or some other person thinks) and relative
(the truth of the statement will depend on what in fact they
do think). The distinction to keep in mind is this: are we
really talking about school itself or how someone feels about
school? Do we intend to describe something about the world
or something about a particular person?

The adage "Beauty is in the eye of the beholder" is a
paradigm example of Naive Relativism. Instead of comparing
the artistic merit of Picasso to that of Walter Keane (the
artist who paints children with very large eyes), we might
just say "Well, I know what I like." Instead of considering
grounds on which we might compare the Budapest String
Quartet with Kiss (a hard rock group who achieved popularity
in the mid-70s), we hear people say: "That's just noise to
me, you can't call that music," or "I just get bored when I
hear stuff like that." Again, it's important to see the distinction

in terms of how the truth will be determined. The Naive Relativist will, in effect, say that aesthetic judgments are really descriptions of the speaker (matters of opinion), that this person likes Picasso, that another likes the Budapest String Quartet and still another likes Kiss.

On the other hand, we can certainly imagine a lively debate on the merits of Picasso as opposed to Keane. We can compare the stylized forms and the functions of each, we can compare the two diverse conceptions of the world, and we can argue which depiction is preferable. In other words, our debate presumes that the works of one artist can be shown to have greater artistic merit than the works of another. Those involved in the debate intend to make a claim about something in the world; they do not intend to simply describe their own subjective states.

But, you might ask, isn't arguing preferability still a matter of personal opinion? For example, I might prefer Keane's mode of presenting persons (they are attractive and not in angular pieces); you might prefer Picasso's political statements. Such preferences are not apparently objective. Our preferences may not be objective, I reply, but surely the pictures are, for they are objects in the world having distinct characteristics. These pictures, in addition, can depict *existing* attitudes *in the world* or attitudes we would like to see exist in the world. For example, Keane captures an idealized concept of children prevalent in our culture: attractive, appealing, helpless, soft and malleable. This attitude existed before Keane's paintings and account, in part, for the popularity of his paintings. The paintings themselves reinforce this attitude, whether or not Keane intended this. The point here is that even something so totally "personal" as one's perception of art has an objective side to it, that when we *assert* our preferences or consider the effect a painting has on us or debate some point about the work, we have entered this objective realm. We are no longer simply describing subjective states of a person; we are now talking about the characteristics of an object in the world.

The same distinction is apparent in ethical debate. In ethics, the moral worth (rightness or wrongness) of an action is considered. This includes "Killing is wrong," "Abortion is right," "One should never deceive another." A Naive Relativist will analyze these statements as being statements about how the speaker feels or what the speaker believes. "Killing is wrong" really means, according to the relativist, that the speaker is horrified by acts of killing or violence, or that "Killing is wrong for you." Again, the truth of the statement is determined by what the speaker feels or believes.

On the other hand, a nonrelativist would point out that if we want to talk about the act of killing itself, or acts of violence or aggression, we are talking about something objective, something in the world, and something that will affect us all. We expect our analysis of aggression to hold true independently of my personal feelings or yours.

But the relativist will insist that we cannot make claims that are truly independent of our personal feelings. To be "a measure of what is and of what is not" is advocating a conception of knowledge as subjective and relative. This means, as we have seen in our examples, that the Naive Relativist will analyze knowledge claims as descriptions of a person rather than as descriptions of the world.

7. Subjective Evidence: A Philosophical Dilemma

Though we may disagree with some of the relativistic interpretations of the above statements, we are quite familiar with the strategy: resolve disagreement by appeal to differences of opinion, belief, feelings on the part of the speakers. In this section, I will talk about what happens philosophically when we make such a move. I will not be evaluating Naive Relativism at this point, but will show, on the one hand, what philosophical position a Naive Relativist will hold, and, on the other hand, how the philosopher from Chapter One sets the stage for Naive Relativism.

In Chapter One, we saw that descriptions of a person were often used as *evidence* for claims about the world. If I want to demonstrate to you that there is a turntable here, I will send you to the appropriate place in the room, have you notice the features of the object before you (a platter, a spindle), I might ask you to activate the turntable, feel the switch, see the record drop and hear the music begin as the arm lowers onto the record. These various sensations, what you see, feel, hear, will prove to you that I am right in claiming there is a turntable here. But these sensations, feelings, beliefs are still "private" to you and to me. Reports of such experiences would be subjective statements because my own states (or yours) will determine the truth of the statement.

Similarly, if I claim to know that the turntable is not in the living room but at the repair shop, I can justify the claim by recalling the events leading up to taking it to the repair shop. "I remember unplugging the turntable and securing the arm, . . ." Notice that even here the evidence I use depends on what *I* remember and on what *I* did.

As we saw in Section 6, we can compare the two types of claims in the following way. One type will talk about something in the world:

O: Here is a turntable. The turntable is at the repair shop.

Another type, used to justify O-statements, will consist of descriptions of the states of a person:

S: I hear music. I see an object having a rotating disc. I recall packing up the turntable.

In other words, I would justify "The turntable is in the repair shop"—an objective or O-statement—by appeal to statements of the type "I recall packing up the turntable"—subjective or S-statements. Here we see the two kinds of statements are very intimately related but still distinct *types* of statements. Even though O-statements will depend upon S-statements for much of their justification, they are not the same kind of statement. As we've seen, O-statements depict things in the world and S-statements depict a person's subjective reponse to this world.

On the other hand, the Naive Relativist wants to say that O-statements are really disguised S-statements. In other words, any claim to knowledge is really a description of this person or that person (not 'person' as an object in the public world, but 'person' as a subject—one who has feelings, beliefs, hopes, desires, expectations, intentions). The Naive Relativist is able to claim that knowledge is subjective by shifting the emphasis (or changing what we are talking about) *from* something in the world *to* subjective states of somebody in the world.

We might feel a bit uneasy with this shift of emphasis. After all, we might not want to abandon the possibility of knowing an "objective" world altogether. Normally there is a clear opposition between the relativist who supports the shift to subjective knowledge and the nonrelativist who defends objective knowledge. However, the nonrelativist philosopher of Chapter One, as we will see, seems to provide the very rationale for such a shift by failing to provide an adequate account of evidence. Such support from the nonrelativist lends enough credibility to this shift of emphasis to make it seem a necessary shift, whatever we might have to give up in knowing an objective world.

Using subjective evidence to justify objective statements has always posed something of a problem. We are all familiar with times we thought something was there when it wasn't. Driving down a stretch of road on a hot day, we sometimes see what appears to be a large puddle ahead or flooding in the road. When we get to that place in the road the pavement is dry and hot. Whereas it is false that the road is flooded, it is true that I see what appears to be flooding ahead. The task for the philosopher is to somehow avoid asserting a false O-statement ("The road is flooded") as knowledge. But the S-statement ("I see what appears to be water on the road") is true and is the kind of statement we need to demonstrate objective knowledge.

In this case, our evidence doesn't "preserve truth." In other words, we would like the truth of the S-statements used as evidence to "carry over" to the O-statement. Ideally there should be no gaps in our chain of evidence. When the S-statements are all true, and there are no gaps in the evidence, it would seem that truth has been "preserved" and the O-statement will be true (i.e., that we cannot be mistaken about what we assert in the O-statement).

The Naive Relativist also sees the possibility of making a false claim, even when the evidential statements are true. But the relativist sees, as well, a fairly straightforward solution. If we want to preserve truth in knowledge and if we can be mistaken about O-statements, then it only makes sense to assert S-statements as knowledge, statements about which we cannot be mistaken. Perhaps "I see what appears to be water on the road ahead" is what we really know.

If we conceive knowledge to be subjective rather than objective, we will no longer have a problem of evidence, says the relativist. If a claim to knowledge is a description of this person or that, the only requirement for truth is that the person *be in* the state they are reporting. It wouldn't even matter if they told the truth about their states, for "my" knowledge would be of my own states, not of yours. In effect the philosopher's emphasis on certainty has backfired here. In defending subjective foundations primarily on the grounds of certainty, the philosopher inadvertently encourages the view that perhaps subjective knowledge is the only real knowledge we can have.

If the philosopher wants to avoid providing such support, the original dilemma must be resolved. The crux of the dilemma lies in a confusion about evidence itself. Because we do want truth to be preserved in O-statements, the philosopher has emphasized the role of truth in S-statements. This gives the impression that *any* true statement will necessarily be good evidence for something or other. But what makes some S-statements good evidence is not just the fact that they are true (though we do want them to be true). What makes some S-statements good evidence is the fact that *they are able to confer* evidence on another statement, i.e., that they can bring us to know something about the world beyond what they themselves assert.

I will appeal to a metaphor to make this point more clearly. I notice that I don't hear any music out of one of my speakers. I prepare to make yet another trip to the repair shop, this time with my speakers. But then I notice that the wires are lying on the floor, detached from a speaker. And I am "informed" that the speaker is not defective, the wires need only to be reattached. That is, one of the things I know about this world is the principle "Speakers must be wired to the amplifier before they will emit sound." This last statement shows, explicitly, the relationship between speakers and the amplifier (that they must be wired properly). Hence it is not just the truth of "I see wires lying on the floor" which allows this S-statement to function as evidence for our O-statement, "The speaker, though not emitting sound, is not defective." The S-statement, in order to justify the O-statement needs the general belief or principle that the speakers and amplifier must be wired together. We'll call this additional statement a G-statement to emphasize the fact that it depicts, in a general statement, the relationship between what we see or hear and what there is in the world: "[Seeing] speakers detached from the amplifier indicates that no sound will come from the speakers when the amplifier is on."

Such statements then are about the world and are objective. At some earlier time, this G-statement must have been itself justified and shown to be a legitimate knowledge claim so that it can now function as a principle which guides us from subjective statements to something in the world.

The philosopher of Chapter One emphasized the need for certainty at the foundations of knowledge. This leaves the relativist with the impression that knowledge can only be subjective (for it seems that we can only be absolutely certain about our own thoughts and feelings). In pointing to the role of G-statements, we are able to show the relativist how to *use* subjective statements as evidence rather than stopping our inquiry into knowledge with them. However, until such general statements are included in our concept of evidence,

Naive Relativism will continue to seem like a reasonable position to take if we wish to preserve truth in knowledge.[2]

8. Different Strokes for Different Folks: Abuses

Whereas we might see the need for subjective knowledge, particularly in the light of existing problems in our concept of evidence, we will take a look in this section to where this could lead us. The primary concern here is to see how a position like Naive Relativism can affect the way we see the world and act in the world.

Naive Relativism is certainly alive and well in the idioms of our ordinary language. "True for you, true for me" is echoed in "To each his own," "Everyone is entitled to their own opinion," "When in Rome do as the Romans do," "Different strokes for different folks," and "Whatever feels good," to cite but a few examples. We use these idioms casually and comfortably. There seems to be little need to ask ourselves what we are really saying. In fact, we might not even consider ourselves relativists when we use the expressions. We might think such idioms are vacuous, silly phrases currently in vogue but soon gone.

If, however, you begin to listen closely to conversations— long talks as well as brief "Hi, how are you?" exchanges— you will begin hearing how much our casual speech is peppered with relativistic expressions. Even though we may not reflect on what we are saying when we use these expressions, we do become accustomed to hearing them and using them. They become a familiar part of our environment. We can expect that just the repetition of such relativistic expres-

---

2. Roderick Chisholm has, thus far, given the most thorough treatment of such "principles of evidence," in *Theory of Knowledge*, 2nd ed. (Englewood Cliffs, N.J.: Prentice-Hall, 1977) and in "On the Nature of Empirical Evidence" in *Empirical Knowledge: Readings from Contemporary Sources*, ed. R. Chisholm and R. Swartz (Englewood Cliffs, N.J.: Prentice-Hall, 1973). It should be noted that Chisholm's use of these principles differs from that described here.

sions *can* produce in the speakers of the language a predisposition to uncritically accept or prefer relativistic positions on the grounds of familiarity (sometimes called "common sense"). We will talk in this section about how this can happen and why I am concerned.

For example, "Different strokes for different folks" is used to explain differences in opinions, preferences and behavior. Jane caps the toothpaste; John leaves it uncapped. They periodically grumble about the other. We might chuckle and seek to appease them with "Different strokes for different folks." Here we are encouraging Jane and John to be a little more tolerant of the other.

Let's consider another case. Smith and Jones have turned their debate to the question of pornography. Smith defends the distribution of any pornography on the grounds that it provides private, erotic pleasure to individuals and doesn't harm anyone. Jones disagrees on the grounds that some pictures depict women (and children) being abused or humiliated, which might encourage or sustain the social view that women (and children) are appropriate objects of abuse and humiliation. If we come along and seek to appease Smith and Jones with "Different strokes for different folks" we are doing more than encouraging them to be more tolerant of one another. We are stopping an important debate and shifting the emphasis of the debate from the question of pornography to descriptions of Smith and Jones.

Here the shift of emphasis becomes more than an academic point, for the consequences of this shift become what I will call the "abuses" of a position like Naive Relativism. For example, the failure to pursue debate and reach a genuine reconciliation will inhibit our efforts to implement solutions to social problems. We might additionally be led to believe that since the different attitudes of Smith and Jones seem fundamental and irreconcilable, the two sides of the debate must likewise be "fundamentally" opposed and irreconcilable. Further, since our attention is directed now towards Smith and Jones and away from pornography, we might conclude that the immediate beliefs, feelings and preferences of a

person are more important (or of greater concern) than what
happens in the public world.

In our use (whether accidental or intentional) of Naive
Relativism, we could find our *habits of reasoning* affected.
The more we "resolve" debate by appeal to something like
Naive Relativism, the less we are called upon to use our
critical judgment. We might, with practice in choosing the
seemingly "easy" form of resolution, begin expecting quick
answers and instant solutions to the various problems that
face us. In other words, we can diminish our capacity to
inquire, probe, question, think beyond the obvious, and to
challenge. In a world where we *are* called upon to judge,
make decisions and evaluate, such losses however small (of
our reasoning skills) can leave us feeling more powerless
than in fact we are.

In using Naive Relativism we might fail to keep in mind
the clear distinction between objective knowledge and subjective knowledge, which can precipitate the following. As
mentioned in Section 6, we may not always distinguish what
Smith thinks from the issue at hand. We may be inclined
to adopt the belief that whatever a person thinks is right,
at a particular time, *is* right. "Smith thinks pornography is
harmless" becomes "Pornography is harmless (for Smith),"
which might carelessly become the assertion "Pornography
is harmless." In other words, we might not think to ask for
the justification or the evidence being used to make this
latter claim. And this claim is an objective claim. However,
with relativistic habits we might overlook the need for the
claim to be justified.

Earlier I made the claim that frequently hearing or using
relativistic idioms could produce in the speakers of the language a predisposition to uncritically accept or prefer relativistic positions on the grounds of familiarity (rather than
on the grounds of its being a more adequate position).
Consider a moral dilemma. You are a student in a class of
three hundred. You feel you have worked hard, but are not
doing well in class. In such a large class, cheating is fairly
easy. Grades are important. You are on your way to law
school and the competition is stiff.

One version of ethical relativism might be: a person must decide for himself or herself what is right or wrong. Here you might say, since I have to decide for myself and since I want a better grade in class, cheating is okay.

Compare this with a version of ethical "absolutism," namely utilitarianism, which says you must act in the long-range interest of all people concerned. Cheating would undermine the practice of fair testing as a means of rating your standing (and that of others) in a particular area. To lose the practice of fair testing does not serve the long-range interest of all people concerned, so you must not cheat.

The point of the comparison is simply to note that ethical relativism sounds more familiar, that it is something we hear more often. This makes it "easier to understand." We don't have to stop and think about what the position asks us to do, as we might with the position of ethical absolutism represented here. The familiarity could lead to the response that the relativistic solution "seems right." But the point is that the solution seems right not because it is right but because it reiterates something already familiar to us.

The position of Naive Relativism does not itself advocate uncritical thinking or withdrawal from problem-solving. I am suggesting, however, that Naive Relativism does lead to such practices, which I am calling the abuses of the position. I consider these things abuses for the following reasons. Diminishing our capacity for critical judgment and evaluation is a *misuse* of our ability to reason, learn and investigate. In failing to seriously address social inequities, for example, we permit continued *mistreatment* of people. And in withdrawing into subjective knowledge, in effect ignoring or not seeking knowledge of a public world, we *deceive* both ourselves and those around us into thinking we are neither responsible for practices in the public world nor capable of changing such practices.

On the other hand, we have also seen that Naive Relativism does seem to address the problems philosophers are having with evidence in showing the truth of objective statements. So long as Naive Relativism *does* seem to address the problems, it will remain firmly entrenched in our language and in our actions. To rid ourselves of the possibility of the abuses discussed above, the confusions with evidence will have to be cleared up before we can show that Naive Relativism does not provide a genuine answer to the philosopher's dilemma.[3]

9. The Problem of Evidence

The two weaknesses cited in Section 7 regarding the analysis of evidence were the overemphasis on certainty (and the guarantee of such certainty with descriptive, subjective statements) and the underemphasis on the rules or principles or general beliefs which transformed a descriptive, subjective statement into a statement *able to confer evidence* on another statement.

I shall not recommend abandoning the quest for certainty as a response to the first weakness. Rather, I should think we only need be reminded that the goal of certainty is certainty with respect to knowledge of the public world in which we live and act, which we affect and are affected by. With such a reminder we fall easily into making the distinction between objective statements and what will justify these statements. In other words, if we keep in mind that evidence functions to *expand* our knowledge and understanding of the world, we will be less likely to see subjective knowledge as a full-blown, genuine body of knowledge. We may use subjective claims as evidence and know these claims to be true; but when we *also* see subjective claims as leading us towards knowledge of an objective world—that 'evidence' requires this dynamic role—we will be less likely to adopt the constraints of a subjective conception of knowledge.

---

3. It is common to reject Naive Relativism on the grounds of logical inconsistency and to cite the logical paradoxes the position generates. Since I'm more concerned here with how this position affects our habits of reasoning and actions in the world, I will simply refer the reader to J. Harrison's article on "Ethical Subjectivism" in the *Encyclopedia of Philosophy*, for a brief review of the logical problems.

The remaining weakness, that of showing how a subjective statement *becomes* an evidential statement, is philosophically more of a problem. Let's return to the pornography debate with Smith defending it as harmless and Jones opposing Smith. It won't be enough for Smith to say "Well I just feel that it's harmless," for Jones will challenge the assertion that it's harmless (not that Smith feels this way). In other words, the truth of Smith's statement "I just feel that pornography is harmless" (true because Smith *does* feel that way) in no way allows us to decide whether or not pornography *is* harmless. Smith's feeling is on par with "I have a headache" in reporting something about Smith. There is nothing to challenge, nothing to decide upon, nothing to agree on. In effect, the Naive Relativist, as we have seen, puts all knowledge claims at this level. That is, knowledge claims are really reports of Smith's or Jones's private beliefs, personal feelings, observations or attitudes.

However, as we have also seen, the *object* of Smith's belief (that pornography is harmless) is something that Jones can and does challenge. Pornography is something in the world that affects everyone in the world, beyond how one person happens to feel about it. How, in this example, can the feelings of one person lead us to a decision about something in the world? The strategy suggested in Section 7, using the example of the speaker wires, might help us here. Briefly, we used the subjective statements:

S: I see wires lying on the floor; I hear no sound from the speakers,

to decide whether or not the speakers were defective. However, the only way I could make a reasonable decision about this was by appealing to the general belief:

G: Speakers must be wired to the amplifier before they will emit sound.

Once I appeal to the G-statement, my S-statments become perfectly good evidence for the objective claim:

O: The speakers are not defective.

If I rewire the speakers to the amplifier and sound is restored, it seems that my O-statement was right. But only when the G-statement *guided me to the connection* between seeing the wires on the floor, not hearing any sound from the speakers and the speakers not working could the S-statement function as evidence. In addition, since my S-statements are true and my G-statement is true, it's quite likely that my O-statement is true as well (and truth has been preserved in this case). If I had gone directly from my S-statement to the objective claim, my evidence would have been much weaker and somewhat questionable.

Can we use the same strategy with the more complex debate between Smith and Jones about pornography? We left the debate at the point of saying that Smith's feeling only tells us about Smith and not about pornography. Jones, however, challenged the object of Smith's feeling: that pornography is harmless. However, it remains unclear just what Smith likes about pornography or even what she takes "pornography" to be. In other words, we cannot proceed with our strategy until we question Smith further about these things.

We saw in Section 8 that Smith's approval of pornography really came down to her desire to encourage the view that private, erotic pleasure should be available and enjoyed by (all) persons. Hence, the subjective reports Smith really is appealing to are:

S: I like to experience erotic pleasure; I feel such pleasure oftentimes when viewing pornography.

The emphasis is on erotic pleasure and is only secondarily on pornography (as a means to erotic pleasure). This distinction is important because, as we saw, Jones also likes to experience erotic pleasure and has no intention of arguing against the pursuit of such pleasure. He happens to object to the manner in which some of this pleasure is sought.

Now that we have identified Smith's primary concern, we can move towards formulating the objective claim she intends to defend. We seem to capture her intent in the following general statement,

G: Feeling pleasure indicates the presence of a pleasurable situation or object (in this case pornography),

or we might even come closer to what she is really saying with

G': Feeling erotic pleasure enhances my life and might well enhance the lives and experiences of others.

Jones, as we will see below, will reject G but accept G'. Since they are in agreement about G', let's see what the S-statements and the G'-statement lead to:

O: Providing erotic pleasure for oneself is desirable.

Rather than terminating inquiry (as did the Naive Relativist by saying that we could not claim knowledge beyond the S-statements), we have opened up a valuable area of discussion: whether or not erotic pleasure is desirable. Smith feels it is and will be able to argue on behalf of that position and perhaps lead us to reflecting on our own attitudes and practices.

Jones wants to broaden the debate to be able to talk about more than just erotic pleasure. Jones's concern is with whether or not we want to associate pleasure with situations in which women (and sometimes children) are depicted as helpless and compromised. By using the previous strategy on Jones's feelings, we will unearth statements that are quite different from Smith's:

S: I (Jones) abhor seeing anyone being debased.
G: Pictures depicting women in bondage, as recipients of aggression, or solely as instruments of another's pleasure (even if they are pictured as enjoying the experiences)

devalue their independence, their dignity and their right
to be a genuine participant in the intimate exchange of
sexual pleasure.

Here, Jones wants to focus the debate on only those cases
of pornography which compromise a person in the ways
suggested. In effect, Jones is promoting the position that all
persons have a right to dignity and self-respect and that
some pornography will diminish one's self-respect. Hence,
Jones is in a position to begin to argue:

O: Everyone has the right to dignity and self-respect,

as well as

O': Pornography which debases women (or children) is harmful and should be censored.

I am not suggesting that the debate should stop here, but
what we have done is to bring the debate to the real issues
in the world which concern both Smith and Jones and affect
them as well as the rest of us. What we have done is to
transform the subjective feelings of Smith and Jones into
statements which direct our attention to practices and attitudes in the world. The feelings by themselves couldn't really
tell us anything about the world or be used to justify objective
claims, even though we could report our feelings in true
statements. We first had to make clear just what the feelings
involved were, then consider which of our general beliefs
would allow these feelings to indicate something in the
objective world.

Well, you might say, the above statement, "Pornography
should be censored," doesn't describe something in the world,
it only describes something *Jones wants* to be in the world.
This question brings us back to the fuzzy area of what to
do with ethical statements. But here Jones seems to be a
nonrelativist: he seems to want to do more than just describe
his own opinion and preference. He wants us to implement
the practice, in the world, of censoring pornography. Of

course Jones still has to argue that such censorship is more justified than noncensorship. But his claim is objective in the sense that there are cases of pornography (pictures, etc.) which depict women as objects of humiliation and these pictures should be withdrawn from circulation, asserts the claim, regardless of what Smith or Jones or anyone else thinks. Jones might well intend his claim to be universal: anyone who takes a thoughtful look at these particular cases will arrive at the conclusion that they should be withdrawn from circulation. Whether or not ethical statements can be successfully shown to be objective and universal is not at issue, however.

Here we are more concerned with *how* subjective statements can turn our attention to the objective world and how they might be able to justify claims about the objective world. To claim that our O-statements are sufficiently justified to be knowledge requires further demonstration of their objectivity and universality (that erotic pleasure *is* desirable for everyone and that everyone *does* have the right to dignity and self-respect). Even the G-statements we appeal to can be scrutinized and brought into the debate for examination.

The points to remember, though, are (1) that only with the addition of true G-statements can subjective statements function as evidence for objective claims and preserve truth, and (2) that the debate is conducted "objectively" in the sense of talking about practices and attitudes *in the world* and which attitudes we would like to see represented *in the world*. This is a far cry from restricting our debate to the feelings of Smith and Jones. But notice, too, that we were very careful to depict as accurately as possible the feelings of Smith and Jones and to make sure the debate represented their real concerns. In this way, the Naive Relativist is shown how subjective statements can be used to talk about the objective world and that knowledge does not have to be restricted to the opinions and feelings of this person or that.

You might, at this point, enjoy analyzing a statement I heard in which Naive Relativism was asserted and was used to stop further discussion. Barbara Walters, popular television news personality, was interviewing Spiro Agnew, Nixon's

Vice-President from January 1972 to October 10, 1973. Referring to the hearings which resulted in Agnew's disbarment, she posed this question: "Were you honest in your testimony?" Agnew replied: "Honesty is different things to different people."[4]

---

4. "20/20," ABC News Magazine, aired on 15 May 1980.

CHAPTER THREE
Context Relativism

10. The Importance of Context: Three Examples

We have just seen how the subjective feelings of Smith and Jones can serve to direct our attention to an objective situation—one which is present in the world and which affects all of us. Rather than restrict knowledge to the feelings and opinions of each person, such feelings or sensations or beliefs can now (when properly used) become evidence for a much larger body of knowledge. This larger body of knowledge will include descriptions of chairs and typewriters, economic recessions and political intrigue, the behavior of physical substances and laws governing the interaction of molecules, as well as descriptions of Smith and Jones.

The subjective feelings of Smith and Jones, on the other hand, are only a very small part of coming to know the world. More important, it seems, is the information we all receive which actually comes from the world. If, for example, I want to sit down, I will look around for a chair. I see a chair. I sit down. I don't just imagine there is a chair, I actually see one and am able to sit on it. This object is "presented" to me, in a sense, as something before me in the world. The truth of the statement "Here is a chair," then, will not depend on whether I've had my eyes checked lately nor does it depend on my mood or my desire to sit down. The truth of the statement is solely determined by whether or not there is a chair here. In other words, a true statement represents or depicts something actually in the world.[1]

Sometimes it seems more difficult to check the truth of a statement: "Smith is certainly angry with Jones today." As I peer at Smith, I don't see evidence of anger, only her usual friendly response as she returns a book. Later in the day, however, I notice she is somewhat cool towards Jones. Perhaps, then, she is angry with Jones.

Many of our statements attempt to represent relations between things or people in the world; we do not just go around describing the objects of our immediate perception such as chairs and typewriters. Even in these more difficult cases, we would want to say that a true statement represents or depicts something actually in the world. In the above example, the statement claims that Smith is, in fact, angry with Jones. Perhaps it is important that I know whether or not this statement is true (since I have planned to ask them both to dinner this evening to discuss curriculum changes and may want to wait until their differences have been resolved). The point is that empirical knowledge isn't just confined to tangible physical objects, but will include situations, events, relationships, practices, attitudes—all of which are in the world much in the way tables and chairs are in the world.

The "context" in which a statement is made obviously has much to do with the truth or falsity of the statement. Our normal understanding of context is to look at the whole situation or background in which something occurs. Perhaps

---

1. This is the position known as the Correspondence Theory of Truth, which says that true statements correspond to facts in the world. There are other positions, but this, I think, comes closest to our everyday expectations of the role of truth. On the other hand, I don't mean to suggest that our everyday expectations are a valid criterion; at this point I am most interested in representing our expectations rather than arguing for a theory of truth.

Smith and Jones frequently disagree. Knowing this I simply wait for things to cool down before asking them to agree on curriculum changes. In the same vein, we will often reread a paragraph in a text to get the exact use of a term or the particular significance of a sentence—what we loosely call getting the meaning from the context. Likewise, quoting "out of context" alludes to the situation in which what someone has said has been misrepresented.

We might say, then, that a true statement will correctly represent the context of utterance—the situation in which the statement is made. "Here is a chair" is true by virtue of the fact that there is a chair before me. "Smith is angry with Jones" will be true if Smith is angry with Jones or false if Smith does not happen to be angry with Jones. "In 1492, Columbus sailed the ocean blue" is true since Columbus was at sea in 1492.

When we cite historical facts, as we've just done, we seem to go beyond anything that would be called a "context of utterance." But what we say ("utter") does accurately represent a particular situation in the world, namely that there was such a person as Columbus who, after considerable preparation, which included the gathering of crews and the building of vessels, was sailing for much of the year 1492 A.D. Hence we can talk about anything that has actually happened in the world, i.e., we can make true claims about such situations, rather than being solely confined to statements about what's happening right at this moment.

The important point for us is that a true statement should represent something in the world, past or present. This "something in the world" might be an object like a chair, or a situation like Columbus's setting sail in 1492, or an economic recession in the United States in 1981, or a relationship like that which exists between Smith and Jones or perhaps, on another level, the bonding of atoms to form molecules, or a general trend like dwindling college enrollments.

We might say that each of these "things" in the world circumscribes boundaries by which we can then assess the truth or falsity of what we say. If you tell me the seat of the green chair is torn, I can look over at the chair and see the tear. If we are watching an episode of "Mork and Mindy" (situation comedy aired 1978–82) on television and you mention the price of tea in China, I will be hard put to make any sense of your train of thought much less assess the truth of what you say. There is nothing by which to measure the accuracy of your claim. If, however, I pick up the business section of the paper and see the report on rising tea prices in China, I am now able to understand the context within which your comment becomes intelligible.

The point that what we say must accurately represent something in the world (if what we say is true) is made by Aristotle using the analogy of a man's existence:

> The fact of the being of a man carries with it the truth of the proposition that he is, and the implication is reciprocal: for if a man is, the proposition wherein we allege that he is is true, and conversely, if the proposition wherein we allege that he is is true, then he is. The true proposition, however, is in no way the cause of the being of the man, but the fact of the man's being does seem somehow to be the cause of the truth of the proposition, for the truth or falsity of the proposition depends on the fact of the man's being or not being.[2]

Being "the cause of the truth of the proposition" is, loosely, what we expect from the context. The tear in the seat of the green chair informs me that what you say is true. To bring in some of the technical vocabulary from Chapter One, we would say that the truth conditions of a statement are given in terms of what is in the world. The conditions—a tear in the seat of the green chair, Columbus at sea in 1492— must be satisfied in order for our statements to be true.

We can, for convenience, call this way of looking at how truth is determined "Context Representation," for a particular thing or event in the world is represented in a true statement.

---

2. Aristotle *Categories* 14b15–22 in *The Basic Works of Aristotle*, ed. R. McKeon (New York: Random House, 1941), p. 35.

Our standard view of knowledge as true, justified belief would be essentially the same as Context Representation, for a true belief will depict something in the world. This way of conceiving truth is not relativistic. Once something has happened we are able to represent it forever after in a true statement. Even though Columbus's sea voyage came to an end, even though Columbus himself died, it remains true that he did live and that he was at sea in 1492. The truth conditions of the statement "In 1492, Columbus sailed the ocean blue" remains stable for the Context Representationist: no matter when the statement is made, no matter where, Columbus must have been at sea in 1492 for the statement to be true.[3]

Context Relativism, on the other hand, will not agree that truth conditions remain fixed after a particular situation has been described. Any statement will have "fluctuating" truth values, says the relativist, true at one time, false at another, or true in one situation, false in another. Though this sounds something like the Context Representationist saying that "Here is a chair" will be true when there is a chair here and false when there isn't, the analysis of the relativist is quite different as is suggested by the following examples.

In the first example, Agatha Christie suggests that variations in the immediate physical surroundings may affect our judgment of a given object:

> He fitted in[to the puzzle], in rapid succession, a small piece
> of a Minaret, another piece that looked as though it was part
> of a striped awning and was actually the backside of a cat,

---

3. To have stable truth conditions means that universality can be demonstrated, for any observer or inquirer will be able to come to the conclusion that Columbus was at sea in 1492. To eliminate the possibility of these conditions changing due to irrelevant variables (e.g., the intelligence of the inquirer, the lighting in which a situation is observed), a clause is added: "Any investigator will conclude that Columbus was at sea in 1492, *ceteris paribus.*" *Ceteris paribus* literally means "All things being equal," such as the availability of documents to any investigator, etc.

and a missing piece of sunset that had changed with Turn-
eresque suddenness from orange to pink.[4]

Here the actual physical characteristic of the puzzle piece
changes from orange (when seen in isolation) to pink (when
seen as part of the sunset). In other words, the relativist
would say, at first the claim "This puzzle piece is orange"
is true, then it becomes false even though we are talking
about the *same* puzzle piece. It would seem, then, that the
truth conditions for this statement vary with the unique
features of the environment (first it was seen alone, then as
part of the sunset); it is the unique features which determine
whether we see the puzzle piece now as orange, now as
pink.

In a second example, the attitudes of an audience may
affect the way a statement is understood. When General
Douglas MacArthur left Corregidor (in the Philippines) he is
reputed to have said "I shall return." The attitudes of those
hearing the statement will determine whether it is taken as
a threat or a promise. That is, "MacArthur threatens to
return" will be true if the audience is hostile to U.S. foreign
policy, false if the audience perceives U.S. foreign policy in
the Philippines as benevolent.

In a third example, knowledge of a person's biography or
personal history is needed to make sense of what he says
or does. A soldier recently returned from active combat might
reach for his rifle upon hearing a loud bang in the next
room. Though his wife might simply go into the next room
to pick up the books that have fallen on the floor, clearly
the statement "Someone believes that the books in the next
room have fallen on the floor" is true with respect to the
wife, false with respect to the soldier.

In each of these cases, the truth of the statement is affected
by variables which seem to be unique to this person, this

---

4. Agatha Christie, *Dead Man's Folly* (New York: Dodd, Mead & Co.,
1947), p. 169.

place or this situation. Our perception of the color of the puzzle piece was radically altered when the puzzle piece was seen "in the context" of the surrounding pieces. MacArthur's statement took on a meaning beyond the simple prediction that he would return. "In the context of" the war and U.S. occupation (and presumably enforcement of pro-U.S. sentiment), MacArthur's statement carried the weight of a threat to dissidents or a promise to sympathizers. To understand the soldier's action of reaching for his rifle, we need to understand the "context" of his recent return from combat.

11. Argument from Uniqueness: The Relativist's Challenge

The relativist utilizes examples like those above to develop the following line of argument:

1. We understand statements in terms of the context in which they are uttered: for instance, when they directly refer to unique features of the physical surroundings, when they appeal to distinct social (historical, etc.) events, when they include aspects of a person's biography, or when they answer a question at hand.

2. We understand statements in terms of the speaker's intentions, as well: connotation, stress, intonation, gesture, facial expression, delivery (tongue-in-cheek, serious) all contribute to the full meaning of a statement.

3. We also understand statements in terms of the relation of the context to the speaker: is the context a familiar one to the speaker or strange? Is the speaker an expert or a novice in this situation? What habits of thought and judgment are brought to this situation? What preoccupations face the speaker—work-in-progress, problems whether personal or professional, obligations, responsibilities?

4. Our assessment of the truth of these statements will involve, then, an appeal to such context-dependent variables.

5. Understanding what a statement means is a condition of knowledge, of assessing the truth of a statement.

6. Therefore, each claim to empirical knowledge depends on knowledge of the context of utterance, knowledge of the speaker's intention, knowledge of the relation of the claim to the context of utterance and speaker. In other words, knowledge is not based on (universal) facts or invariable states of affairs, but on claims that are dependent on the idiosyncracies of each particular situation.

The plausibility of this line of reasoning lies in the fact that we all depend, to some extent, on such variables in seeking to understand something. The "changing" color of the puzzle piece seems to depend on its location in this particular puzzle. The truth of MacArthur's "promise" to return will vary with the political sentiments of the audience. Also a very different interpretation might be given MacArthur's statement if it is directed to his wife: she may understand that he will be home for dinner. The ordinary event of books falling on the floor was viewed by the soldier as the extraordinary situation of enemy intrusion into his apartment.

More subtly, we are given distinct clues about how to take a statement from the demeanor of the speaker. A popular form of humor is to put down another person, the twinkle in the speaker's eye supposedly informing the recipient not to take the utterance seriously but as a demonstration of affection. Sagging shoulders and a weary expression belie a friend's assurance that all is well. A raised eyebrow tells us of a skeptical attitude. Our language is deeply enriched by the range of nonverbal accompaniment to our statements. Why, then, asks the relativist, should we ignore such important variables by insisting on universal truth conditions? Facial expressions and delivery of a statement cannot be duplicated from utterance to utterance, context to context.

We also need to recognize, says the relativist, that no person enters a conversation or situation free from habits, preoccupations and interests. Let's say that a student comes to my office to talk about rewriting a paper on the individual's moral obligation to the state. The conference will proceed more smoothly if I am attuned to the fact that writing is a difficult and still awkward mode of expression for this student, that his relationship to authority (whether to persons such as parents and teachers or to institutions such as school or the government) is a source of conflict for him, that the student is quite distracted by memories of a party the night before and is hoping to run into someone he met there at the student union as soon as he leaves my office, that he might well be wondering what he's doing in school at all.

Similarly, students seem to expect teachers to function as teachers outside the range of normal academic concerns: a teacher often sees panic and discomfort in the faces of students encountered in the grocery store or neighborhood bar. Because of this underlying conception (fear) of teachers, a student is prevented from hearing in the lectures the instructor's curiosity, the instructor's demand for relevance from the material, and his/her belief that the material can benefit a person's life—all concerns shared by the student and teacher alike. With so many variables contributing to the meaning of a statement, says the relativist, how can we possibly think that truth conditions can remain the same through differing contexts?

Context Relativism appears in ethics as "Situation Ethics." Here the position is that situations are *unique* and that knowledge of a moral solution can only be determined relative to that particular situation:

> Ethical problems arise in the changing contexts of persons and events within which we live. We make our choices and act . . . in situation. [We must be] sensitive to the special characteristics and requirements of each problematic situation, to the distinctive needs of the persons involved. . . .[5]

In other words, the right action depends on or is relative to the special or unique characteristics of the situation.

---

5. C. Eugene Conover, *Personal Ethics in an Impersonal World* (Philadelphia: Westminster Press, 1968), pp. 48–49.

Let's return to the moral dilemma of the student in the last chapter, namely, whether or not to cheat on the final exam. The student, in effect, considers each of the variables cited—stiff competition for law school, effort in class, the fact that he probably won't be caught—to be the "special" needs of this particular situation. The student here will conclude that "Cheating is okay," on the grounds that he needs to maintain competitive grades and will not be caught given the size of the class.

In other areas, Context Relativism appears with any claim of uniqueness (when the uniqueness qualifies only some people as able to know or understand what is being said). Haven't we all relayed a humorous incident only to find much of the humor absent in our description. "It was funny at the time," we say somewhat apologetically. "At the time" could be the particular delivery of a joke or a unique or unusual juxtaposition of events. For the relativist, the fact that this is not reproducible (in this case, that much of the humor is lost) shows the dependence of a statement on the unique variables of the context.

Likewise, "As a member of the white majority, you can't possibly understand the problems of oppression" claims that membership in a nonwhite minority provides a unique perception or understanding of oppression. This understanding is thought to be inaccessible (that is, nonreproducible) to whites. In a similar vein, appeals to "national security" provides a whole range of examples. "To disclose this information (which appears about you in FBI files) will jeopardize national security." Only certain officials, presumably, are uniquely suited to having the information; apparently only they can be counted on not to jeopardize national security. We heard frequently enough, as well, during the Watergate investigations, how "national security" exempted some individuals from adhering to the constraints of our laws. Presumably their unique access to information put them outside the constraints to which the rest of us are subject.

The relativist's point about the nonreproducibility of the circumstances directly challenges the concept of knowledge as true, justified belief. In Section 5 of Chapter One, we said that justified belief could be shown to be universal (and hence qualify as a knowledge claim) if the chain of evidence could be duplicated by anyone in similar circumstances. (That is, if I stand in your living room I will see the same turntable that you see.) But the relativist denies the possibility of genuine duplication. In other words, our Context Relativist has been saying that knowledge can't be objective and universal in the manner represented in Chapter One. Though statements can be objective in the sense of representing something in the world, the relativist says that objective statements are really "uniquely descriptive" statements about a particular situation in the world at a particular time. That is, such statements cannot be universal. Since objective statements are unique descriptions, emphasizes the relativist, their meaning and conditions for truth will vary radically from situation to situation.

12. Philosophers at Work

In one sense, as briefly mentioned above, it is a truism to say that knowledge is relative to the context of utterance. What is before us in the world is, in a broad sense, part of the context or circumstances within which a statement is meaningful. If we are sailing in my small sloop and I say "Here is a typewriter" you might begin wondering about my tolerance for sun. This perfectly good statement is far more appropriately made in my office. Does this mean that we will have to accept the analysis of the Context Relativist?

I think not. In this section I will show that the Context Relativist is claiming something very different from the Context Representationist, the nonrelativist. The nonrelativist will be able to show *universal* truth conditions and still account for the frequent variations in our experience. Compare the accounts of context in this section with those of the last section.

In the following quote, Ernest Sosa suggests that belief (and hence adequate justification of the belief) might need to include reference to features of the context:

> "Jupiter is too far away" [can be ambiguous]. ... Whether Jupiter is too far away depends on the context, and not just because it depends on the physical position of the speaker or thinker, but also because it depends on the question under consideration. If the question is what bodies will strongly affect the initial course of our spaceship then maybe Jupiter is too far, while still it is not too far if the question is rather how far we can go with our fuel supply.[6]

Though we have one statement, "Jupiter is too far away," it seems as if there are two distinct sets of conditions under which our statement will be true, i.e., that it is the *same* statement uttered in two different contexts, which yield two different truth values. No, suggests Sosa, this is not just one statement with two readings, this is two different statements:

A: Jupiter is too far away to affect the course of our spaceship,

and

B: Jupiter is not too far away to reach with our fuel supply.

It seems, then, that the relativist may be exploiting an avoidable ambiguity of some statements. Since we are not always precise and explicit in everything we say, we might well assert what appears to be a sentence with fluctuating truth values when in fact there may be two distinct statements involved.

Using the analogy of "Jupiter is too far away," perhaps we can resolve the problem of the fluctuating truth values

---

6. Ernest Sosa, "Propositional Attitudes *De Dicto* and *De Re*," *Journal of Philosophy* 67 (1963), 894. I have appropriated Sosa's example for the purposes of this discussion; he is examining a very different question from ours in the article.

of our examples in Section 10 of this chapter as well as the "problematic" statements which gave us trouble in Chapter One (the statements about this being *my* office, that being *your* turntable, statements which could not be asserted universally). Perhaps we could make explicit the troublesome (or unique) feature of the context which affects the truth value. Hence, "This puzzle piece is orange" may not have to be true at one time but false at another. When the puzzle piece is fitted into the puzzle, we should say "The orange puzzle piece looks pink when surrounded by yellow."[7]

When we bring the unique feature of the context into our statement—the feature which accounted for the change in truth value—the "new" statement will have to be shown to be objective and universal before we can claim knowledge. "The orange puzzle piece looks pink when surrounded by yellow" is objective in representing (or asserting) relations between colors in the world and how they are perceived. Our "new" statement is universal, for *anyone* who surrounds a small patch of white-pigmented orange with yellow will see that the orange patch appears pink. We are, then, able to demonstrate the universality of the "unique" and "nonreproducible" (according to the relativist) situation.

Similarly, "This is my office" is freed from ambiguity if we simply say "This is Gifford's office." Anyone can identify an office located here and can discover that it is occupied by a person named Gifford. Likewise, "I am standing in my living room" becomes "nonrelativized" when we say "Brown is standing in his living room."[8]

---

7. More precisely, orange will only be affected in this way when the orange shade contains white pigment; orange that is created solely by the mixture of red and yellow will not appear pink when surrounded by yellow.

8. Sentences containing references to "I" or "here" or "now" are referred to as "indexicals," for their truth will be relative to the speaker or context. For a more comprehensive description of the problems these sentences involve, the interested reader should review the article entitled "Indexical Signs, . . ." in the *Encyclopedia of Philosophy*.

In other words, the reason that these sentences and the examples in Section 10—the changing color of the puzzle piece, MacArthur's "promise" to return and the soldier's reaching for his rifle—seemed to support Context Relativism, might well be that their formulation is ambiguous. When we are explicit in the manner suggested by Sosa, the need to "relativize" the truth of a statement is eliminated. The relativist's case seems to fall apart when we can show that the conditions for truth are *reproducible*. The perception of [white-pigmented] orange as pink when surrounded by yellow is not unique to this situation or that observer. Anyone can experiment with color and make the same claim. (The Gestalt movement in psychology utilized this analysis of context, thus retaining the universality of their claims.)

If this is right, then our two remaining examples should no longer be a problem. MacArthur's "I shall return" will be heard as either "MacArthur threatens to return" or "MacArthur promises to return." The first will be true when the audience is antagonistic to MacArthur's presence; the second will be true when the audience is sympathetic to his presence. Anyone can understand, for example, that hostility towards MacArthur or U.S. foreign policy would most likely be manifested in hearing MacArthur's statement as a threat. This doesn't mean that everyone must disapprove of U.S. foreign policy; it only means that anyone can understand when MacArthur's statement would be heard as a threat. This is all that is needed to show universality.

Similarly, "Someone believes the books have fallen on the floor" was shown to be true with respect to the wife, false with respect to the soldier. It would not be very satisfying here, however, to just turn the statement into simple descriptions: "The wife believes the books have fallen on the floor" and "The soldier believes a shot has been fired in the next room." The reason the example was puzzling in Section 10 was that it was so "out of context" for the soldier to reach for a rifle, so surprising that he would think a shot had been fired. Once we understand his recent experiences in combat, we nod and say "Of course." We understand, now, a continuity which makes his belief and his action reasonable and not at all surprising.

It is this point about continuity which brings us to the confusion involved in the position of Context Relativism. Showing the universality of a statement and turning one statement into two will not dispel some of the misunderstandings that keep relativism so popular and appealing. I will use an example from Hegel, a nineteenth-century philosopher, to introduce this point:

> What is the Now? We reply, for example, the Now is nighttime. . . . [W]rite that truth down. . . . If we look again at the truth we have written down, look at it *now*, at this *noon-time*, we shall have to say it has turned stale and become out of date.
> . . . The Now is simply day-time which has many Nows within it—hours. A Now of that sort, again—an hour—is similarly many minutes . . . and so on. Showing, indicating, pointing out [the Now] is thus itself the very process which expresses what the Now in truth really *is*: namely a result, or a plurality of Nows all taken together.[9]

This quote brings to mind one, still popular, "proof" that knowledge is as transient as the world it seeks to describe. As soon as you have made a "true" statement about something in the present, a clever relativist sometimes "argues" that the statement has already ceased being true, for the present you have described has already become the past.[10] The confusion which sustains relativism is this: If we say "Now it is night and now it is day" we have expressed a contradiction, for presumably the "now" refers to the same moment. But "now" cannot refer to the same moment, for

---

9. G.S.F. Hegel, *The Phenomenology of Mind*, trans. J. B. Baillie (New York: Macmillan, 1955), pp. 151, 157. I am not intending to represent Hegel's position but am merely using his example to help make my point.

10. Though still a popular line of reasoning, the argument seems to have been originally proposed by Cratylus, a contemporary of Socrates in Athens.

with each utterance a new moment has come into being. So no matter how accurately you describe the present, the immediate moment or situation, no matter how true your statement might be when formulated, it becomes obsolete and the truth of the statement fades as quickly as the moment you tried to describe. Hence, says the relativist, seeking stable truth conditions for our knowledge claims will be a futile enterprise.

But, says Hegel, your preoccupation with the immediate and the uniqueness of this moment blinds you to the process of coming to know the world *through* this moment. When we take the Nows together, as a whole, we see a continuity from one moment to the next. It is the *continuity* of the Nows taken together, *not* just what we can say or know about this particular moment, that enables us to know the world we live in.

"Showing," "indicating" and "pointing out" characteristics of the present, of the Now, enables us to know—to become acquainted with—stable, enduring features of our familiar world. The relation of one moment to the next provides a context, if you will, within which we construct our lives: we carry out meaningful action (plan what we will do and are able to realize our plan), exchange information about the world with others, and take for granted the stability and continuity of the world. It is this continuity, says Hegel, which allows us to understand a world beyond our immediate experiences. (Think here of how little the Naive Relativist would know if limited to knowledge of what s/he thinks or feels.)

The surprising action of the soldier enables us to become acquainted with delayed psychological responses to high stress or life-threatening situations. That there are differing interpretations of MacArthur's statement introduces us to political sentiments of Philippinos during World War II. The changing color of the puzzle piece enables us to explore principles of color perception. We are, in each case, led to important and illuminating features of the world. We can investigate and thereby increase our understanding of our familiar world. We are, in other words, able to increase our body of empirical knowledge (which can still be characterized as objective and universal). In relativizing the examples from Section 10, we would not be led to such fruitful investigation.

Will the strategies suggested by Sosa and Hegel work as well for ethical statements and moral dilemmas, such as whether or not to cheat on an exam? These strategies require both that the truth conditions for the statement be universal *and* that the seemingly unique features of the statement be generated by some situation or practice in the world. The student facing the dilemma of cheating might feel that s/he can fulfill both conditions with the statement "Anyone in this large class facing stiff competition to law school should cheat." It is asserted as a universal claim and points to an existing situation in the world, the student might argue.

But giving a statement universal form isn't enough to make its truth conditions universal. What allowed us to universalize our problematic statements about the puzzle piece, MacArthur and the soldier was making explicit the "question under consideration," as Sosa put it. If we are careful to respond to the relevant question (with correct information) our statement will be true (and the truth conditions stable): "Jupiter is not too far away to reach with our fuel supply." If we don't accurately represent the proper question, our statement might well be false (and the truth conditions fluctuating): "Jupiter is not too far away to reach with our supplies." When the caterer, upon hearing this, stops packing food, the statement will be false and the crew will soon get hungry.

The question under consideration for the student is "Will cheating enable me to acquire the skills and information offered by this particular class?" In answering this question, the student will most likely conclude "To acquire the skills and information offered by a particular class, one should not cheat." This statement is objective in that it correctly identifies something in the world (namely, that the practice of cheating will not fulfill the conditions of learning), and it is universal, for anyone considering this dilemma will come to the same conclusion, that cheating cannot promote learning. The anxiety about admission to law school or the possibility of failure in this class, Hegel might say, blinds this student to the real question under consideration. Rather, Hegel might continue, these "unique" features should direct the student's awareness to the need to study, to seek help or to consider the decision to pursue an education.

Our preoccupation with the "unique" and immediate sense of "now" promotes, as well, a too narrow concept of change as radical departure and innovation. When we only see the present as unique and nonreproducible, any subsequent situation will have to be seen as radically different, itself unique and nonreproducible, and sometimes random or arbitrary. Hence, claims the relativist as we have seen, knowledge will be as fleeting and as transient as each situation it depicts. Evidence of transient "knowledge" is all around us, continues the relativist. We watch vital cities decay, humans land on the moon, and Newton's laws supplanted. Where, then, is the fixed and immutable knowledge the nonrelativist seems to advocate? Where, then, is the stable and permanent world such knowledge depicts?

If we were to read only popular magazines and supplements to the Sunday paper, knowledge might indeed seem to be temporary, lasting (for some writers) the duration of a decade. We read about the "innocent" fifties, the "rebellious" sixties and the "Me" decade of the seventies. Each decade is described as unique and unusual. The novel features of the period (as seen by the writer) are culled, simplified and enlarged. It is the job of the journalists to sensationalize changing fashions, trends, fads, styles, attitudes. The emphasis is on change as novel departure or innovation. The more radical the change, the greater the sales of the magazine. This cultivated preference for rapid obliteration of the past (even the immediate past) I will call the "Sunday Supplement Syndrome": extreme emphasis on change and innovation, with particular attention given to whatever can be sensationalized.

I am not opposed to change or development, but the Sunday Supplement Syndrome misrepresents change and promotes a rather odd conception of knowledge as fleeting and transient. "Change" refers to variation, alteration, modification, deviation or transformation. In looking more closely at just what this means, we see that change is more a continuous process than radical departure.

Usually *something* is changed, altered or transformed. That is, if I change the tire on my car or paint the walls of my apartment, the car and the walls undergo alteration but remain my car and my apartment. The change will bear some physical as well as logical connection to the original: I can still find my car in the parking lot.

Change may be obvious, as in painting my walls, or it may be less visible. Even when not apparent, though, most change is still part of a continuity: the practice of using public bodies of water as a disposal for chemical waste would, of course, produce marked changes in the water from the outset. But it was not until the Cuyahoga River in Ohio caught fire in 1969 that we began to take note of the changes.

Directed change, as in the actions I perform daily, modify my world in specific ways and usually fit an existing need. Similarly, the products of our technology modify our world and respond to social needs (or create new ones). To a greater or lesser degree, each change affects the shape of the public world. This was clearly the case when television was introduced into homes. Not only were the entertainment habits of families altered, but social practices (such as the protocol of visiting) were affected. Patterns of thought would change, as well, as consumers became more accusomed to hyperbolic advertising.

Less frequently does change fully disrupt and alter the structure of our experience. Victims of crime, accident or war will usually feel this sort of full disruption; that is, their lives will be unable to proceed in the same manner as earlier. Though these cases do *not* constitute the norm, our discussion of the changes around us often emphasizes the unusual or startling features rather than the conditions leading to this situation: national reporting of the Cuyohaga had this "right out of the blue" character even though local news coverage of pollution in various parts of the country had been going on for ten years. (The news was received in this manner as well, suggesting that the Sunday Supplement Syndrome afflicts the reader and the journalist alike.)

Context Relativism gains much popular support and use from our tendency to sensationalize any alteration in our world. It's a natural step to take from seeing only the unique features in a situation to thinking that knowledge can't be universal. One very strong appeal of Context Relativism is that it does sound very much like an account of the radical and seemingly arbitrary changes that appear in the world daily (or are daily reported in our news coverage). The confusion which Hegel sought to dispel was mistaking "universal" with "never changing." That is, when the relativist heard that a statement had to be shown to be objective and universal to be taken for knowledge, it appears that the relativist thought that what we were saying about the world itself would never, or must never, change. This would be like saying, to oversimplify, that because I claim there is a chair here, the chair must remain here forever after if my statement is to remain true.

The fact that the "Nows all taken together" reveal the continuity of the world, reveal the relation between this moment and the next, enables us to understand change as growth and development, as cause and effect, as intelligible modification and transformation. An acorn doesn't open its shell to a full-blown oak tree, nor did the telephone rudely awaken Bell one night with its incessant ringing. Most change and innovation is characterized by gradual development and growth, the causes identifiable, the effects predictable. That we often fail to recognize the small stages of development is not a characteristic of change but of those who observe the world.

13. Subject and Object

The popular Context Relativist has brought us to the point of reviewing our concept of "objective." We began this chapter by suggesting that objects and events in the world "present" themselves to us and are, in some way, the "cause" of the truth of our statements about the world. This means that the objects and events in the world, their relations to other things and how they can behave (i.e., the ways they can change or be changed) are seen as distinctly independent of human perception, desires, intentions and the like.

The paradigm of this conception of "objective" is heard in Jack Webb's classic line in the old TV show *Dragnet*: "The facts, ma'am, just the facts," delivered deadpan and in a monotone. Normally, however, we think of "objective" as "unbiased," "free of personal opinion," or "neutral." We expect judges to be objective, to leave their personal preferences at home and review a case solely on its merits. Reporters like to think of their investigation as objective— neutral in describing facts without judgment. We would like teachers and employers to be objective, to judge our work fairly, without appeal to whether or not they like us and to be unaffected by the concerns of their own lives.

What is more difficult to understand is how attitudes of people, practices in the world arising from human preference, and values can be thought to be objective. That these things are observable in our world, that they have distinct and recognizable characteristics, that they are part of our environment, that they are embodied in our institutions (e.g., schools, laws) and that they affect the world qualifies attitudes, practices and values to be a legitimate part of the public, objective world. For example, economic recessions are characterized by high unemployment and high interest rates, among other things. (That is, even though "economic recession" might be called something like a human interpretation of a situation, it has tangible characteristics—unemployment, interest rates—which exist independently of an observer.)

More problematic, perhaps, is seeing how an attitude could be called objective. Racism, for example, is characterized by a belief in the inferiority/superiority of people solely on the basis of their racial or ethnic origins. Since racism is a belief, you might say, it has to be held by a person and hence would be subjective, not objective. When this belief becomes recognizable in our world apart from particular people, when such a belief is sustained in law (in this case the old "Jim Crow" laws would be an example) and justified by various social practices (continued controversy over integrated schools and busing), this belief has become an attitude in the public world. Of course it's easier to see a chair as an object than something like an attitude. But an attitude can exist in the world apart from what you or I think, can be distinctively recognized by any observer, and can affect the course of events in the public world. This is why judges can arbitrate charges of racism, reporters can investigate cases of racism, and teachers can reveal the attitudes giving rise to racist practices.

But there is no question that the lines of objectivity become less distinct in these borderline cases. Much of the world, of course, is easily seen as existing independently of human determination: we don't provide ourselves with the onslaught of neuro-physiological stimulation which forms the core of any present perceptual field (what we see, hear, smell, taste or touch around us at any given time). But, as the Context Relativist has argued and as we see in the above examples, this does not capture all the features of the objective world. (And, the relativist reminds us, knowledge claims are supposed to be able to depict *all* the characteristics of the objective world.)

In Section 10 we saw how *subjective* variables affect our experience of the world, whether these variables were physical (as in color perception), political, or psychological. In Section 11, the Argument from Uniqueness demonstrated our dependence on subtleties of language and expression to be able to fully grasp the significance of a statement. (In the same vein, we should note that the use of metaphor, imagery, and irony, for example, can convey a more profound claim, oftentimes, than a direct statement of a point.)

Sosa and Hegel offered the means of incorporating these context-variables into our knowledge claims without sacrificing universality. But these strategies can only accomplish so much. How, for example, can we incorporate into our knowledge claims the vast contribution made by artists, poets and musicians? We saw in Section 12 that human intention has something to do with change in the objective world: we can create and modify objects and situations in this world;

we are an "objective" part of the world of others (including the world of other species and organisms). Doesn't this intricate involvement with the objective world somehow make us a part of what we mean by "objective"?

One traditional response to this inquiry is to appeal to an "invariable core" of our experience. This "core" of experience is whatever cannot be altered by human concerns or human imagination or human intentions; usually it is thought to be a sensory core—the neuro-physiological stimulation we receive from objects before us. This seems to be the only area, some argue, where human intervention will not change the nature of the experience; hence, this alone can lead us to what is in fact in the empirical world (or at least should constitute the foundations of empirical knowledge).[11] But this certainly doesn't look anything like the empirical world we live in, nor does such a sensory core seem capable of accounting for such things as poetic irony which does seem to assert (or bring our attention to) very real aspects of the world and of our experience.

Even though Context Relativism can't offer an adequate account of knowledge, it has brought to our attention some very compelling features of our experience, which, if we want our body of knowledge to be *complete*, should be included in our claims to knowledge. Even in our review of a nonrelativist's depiction of change, we see considerable human presence in the very constitution of the objective world. Perhaps, then, our concept of "objective" will have to be carefully and cautiously expanded to include this "intentional" character of our experience as well as the purely

---

11. This is the position known as "empiricism," sometimes called British empiricism since the English philosophers David Hume, John Locke, and George Berkeley were the most influential advocates of the position. We will not here debate the merits or demerits of empiricism or even go into much technical detail about it; its influence, however, is felt in our mode of conducting scientific investigation and appears as well in our everyday view of the world.

physical character of our neuro-physiological processes.[12] Our concern in this book is not so much how this is to be done but to see if knowledge claims can still be shown to be objective and universal if any intentional component is introduced.

First of all, we need to review what an intentional component to our analysis of "objective" might be. Some of the suggestions made by the relativist in this chapter (beyond the explicit contextual variables) include such things as nuance, gesture, the "history" of a situation (e.g., Smith and Jones's frequent disagreements), the significance of an object or a situation to an observer (e.g., your pride in acquiring your turntable) as well as our direct and intentional manipulation of the world (e.g., painting my walls yellow), our indirect and unintentional effect on the world (e.g., pollution of our water supply, thinning the protective ozone layer in our atmosphere), or generating practices from attitudes (e.g., racism). It does seem reasonable to try to include in our account of knowledge the rich and varied character humans impress on the world as well as bring to their experience of the objective world.

Given our discussion thus far, we will be able to retain the universality of our knowledge claims so long as the truth conditions of a statement are reproducible, that is, so long as any observer viewing this situation can make the same claims I make about it, so long as my experience, so to speak, can be reasonably duplicated by any other observer here. This can be a check on the objectivity of my statement as well, for if any other observer reports seeing the same things I do, I feel assured that an object or situation in the

---

12. The philosophical tradition of phenomenology has perhaps made the most systematic attempt to incorporate this "intentional" feature of our experience into our knowledge claims. This position is classically represented in the works of Husserl, Heidegger and Merleau-Ponty. For interested readers, a fascinating look at our perception of space (from a phenomenological perspective) can be found in Patrick Heelan's *Space, Perception and the Philosophy of Science* (Berkeley: U. of California Press, 1982). Again, we will not present details of the position here.

world genuinely has the characteristics I see. However, given the variety of human response, the effect of personal history on how I will construe a situation, my interests and concerns which are distinctly not universal, how can we modify our conception of objectivity without giving up universality as well?

On the other hand, even with the diversity of my response and perception, the extent to which I can transform the world is limited by the object itself. I can neither turn an acorn into an oak tree overnight nor can I reverse gravitational pull. It is interesting to note that as I increase my knowledge of the world, I increase my ability to transform the world: genetic splicing techniques produce hybrids capable of rapid growth, the use of powerful engines can resist gravitational pull. The objective world, in other words, does not remain static, just waiting for us to discover its various properties and depict them in knowledge claims. Many of its essential characteristics change so that the world described by Socrates in knowledge claims is not wholly the same world we would describe today (e.g., the presence of fluorocarbons in the ozone layer).

Just as the artist's display of a painting becomes part of the objective world as does the U.S. recession in 1981, so too does each and every alteration become part of the objective world *so long as it is capable of "presenting itself" to any observer*. For example, one criterion I find useful in judging a work of art (and which seems to account, in part, for why I will like one work over another) is whether the artist changes my perception of the world. In other words, an artist "sees" something in the world that s/he represents in the most appropriate manner to convey this "observation" (whether by reproducing an image with photographic accuracy or by stylized means, e.g., Van Gogh's later paintings depicting a dense, pulsating rhythm emitting from rigid objects). I am able to see more of the objective world in this way, just as I find that learning about atomic and molecular bonding promotes a certain fascination with physical objects.

To avoid misunderstanding, I have said that any characteristic of the objective world must be *capable* of "presenting itself" to any observer. My untrained eye may miss seeing Chagall's reverent attitude in his paintings, my naive beliefs may inhibit seeing important aspects of human relationships characterized by James Joyce in his writings, just as my former ignorance of molecular theory limited my interest in physical objects to where I could sit or put my books. Because these things that I may miss are in the world, are attributes of objects and events in the world, and can be represented accurately (even if I need instruction to be able to assess the accuracy of the representation), they are capable of becoming a part of our body of empirical knowledge.

We can depict these (changing) features of the world in statements having universal truth conditions; the truth conditions will be given in terms of what is in the world, and any observer will be able to understand what the conditions are and to determine whether the conditions are satisfied in the world (even if the observer needs special training to do so). Unless my unique and personal observation of the world can be either transformed into a public, objective statement (and put to the test of being confirmed or discarded by others in the world), or prompts some action which does alter the public, objective world, such private observations will remain genuine idiosyncrasies of a situation, nonreproducible variables of the context, and hence not capable of representation in our claims to knowledge.

What we see here, then, is not so much a radical alteration in our philosophical conception of "objective" but a means of dispelling some confusion in our ordinary, everyday use of "objective." We are in a better position to relinquish the conception of objective as "just the facts, ma'am" to an appreciation of the rich and diverse character of the objective world. In addition, we are able to accept and assess a wider variety of knowledge claims (all the while keeping the characteristics of objectivity and universality) to include the many "nonscientific" insights offered to us through the mediums of poetry, fiction, music, to name a few.

We can summarize the contrasting analyses of the Context Relativist and the Context Representationist in this way. The Context Relativist insists that claims to knowledge are really unique descriptions of the world at a particular time and place. Since they are unique, the truth conditions are not reproducible, hence knowledge claims cannot be shown to be universal. Our nonrelativist philosophers have suggested, on the other hand, that these supposedly unique statements reveal to us a reasonably stable and predictable world which undergoes change (historical, technological, etc.). Knowledge claims describe such a world and can be shown to be universal because of our ability to reproduce and understand their conditions of satisfaction.

In other words, cities decay under specific social and economic conditions, humans land on the moon when adequate means (transportation, biological maintenance, etc.) are available, Newton stretched our understanding of the empirical world by formulating laws of nature, thus providing us with new conceptual skills to be able to explore further. How could investigation have proceeded if Newton had concluded that gravity is relative to apple trees?

14. It All Depends on What You Mean: Abuses

If the Context Relativist insists on the position of claiming that each and every situation is unique, certain very familiar (and abusive) practices will be encouraged. The abuse is illustrated vividly in our use of the phrase "It all depends on. . . ." In this section I will discuss three popular uses of this phrase.

The first use attempts to resolve debate or argument with "It all depends on what you mean by such-and-so," "It all depends on how you define your terms," or "It all depends on semantics." Presumably, "it" refers to the truth of a claim or to the point which will settle the debate.

Consider a discussion between Smith and Jones, this time asking whether or not our legal system preserves justice. There are many ways to investigate this question. They could list examples of just court decisions and see how often these occur. They could begin by describing what they take justice to be and then apply the description to specific examples. They could consider the social function of the legal system and ask whether this function promotes justice.

No matter how they approach the question, they need some understanding of what "justice" refers to. But notice that this understanding is in the service of evaluating current practices in the legal system.

Now suppose I enter the debate just when Smith and Jones are vehemently disagreeing about the extent to which "white collar crime" is punished. Smith argues that street crimes are more frequently and more severely prosecuted; hence, an injustice is being done to law breakers of an economic class lower than that of white collar workers. Jones argues that the reason there is less prosecution of white collar workers is that there are fewer such crimes, what crimes there are don't really injure or harm others, and white collar workers are good upstanding citizens; hence it is only just that street crimes receive more severe penalties and closer attention.

Suppose I say to Smith and Jones, "Well your whole debate simply turns on how you define 'justice.' If you define it as 'equal protection and equal prosecution under the law,' then Smith is right. If you define it as a 'reward or return on the way you live your life rather than on a single act,' then Jones is right. You really have nothing to argue about." This is what I would call an abuse of the reasonable practice of explicating the key terms of an argument. We should define our terms to remove ambiguity in the discussion and to allow genuine investigation and understanding to proceed. But to suggest that a definition is the *sole* means of resolving debate is to suggest that the issue under discussion involves nothing more than a linguistic ambiguity.

If I convince Smith and Jones that their argument is mere verbal disagreement, I haven't really helped them settle anything. Their investigation was uncovering specific features of the judicial system that we all need to consider if we are concerned about justice. I would want to argue that this is more than sophisticated word play. I would argue that the debate promotes a genuine understanding and recognition of an objective situation in our contemporary world.

Similarly, another abuse is frequently heard in justifying our actions. "It all depends on how you were raised" is a facile generalization of the sound belief in psychology that events and associations from our childhood affect our present behavior. Many of our actions and thoughts have significance beyond the scope of the immediate circumstances. Very often we can change a habit or choose to act more effectively once we correctly identify the early symbolic meaning attached to a behavior or belief.

However the generalization "It all depends on how you were raised"—here, "it" refers to what you do or believe— is not used to promote understanding of our actions nor is it used to seek resolution to specific problems. "I was raised to believe women should serve men" (hence it is all right for me to ignore the needs and desires of my wife or girlfriend) is such a generalization; it is largely used to excuse a person's behavior. Or "I can't help what I am (what I do, what I believe)," or "That's just the way I am" are, in effect, trivial explanations of behavior and justifications for abdicating responsibility for one's actions. Fixating on a *single* "explanation" for what one does, reducing a debate to the use of a *single* term is an extreme parody of the Context Relativist's emphasis on the uniqueness of any set of circumstances.

"It all depends on your point of view" and "It all depends on the situation" are often given to resolve debate (though in a slightly different fashion than in the first case). The issues being debated may vary widely. We could be discussing the political efficacy of taking hostages or the best means of seeking the release of hostages. We could be talking about conservation of natural resources or fair distribution of limited resources. Whatever the issue, the resolution will affect our action and the steps we will take to bring about the desired end. The issues are about situations and practices *in the world* that affect *all of us*. If, instead of pursuing an investigation of these questions, we accept the recommendation of the relativist that the resolution depends on one's point of view, then we are likely to see the course of events in the world as arbitrary or determined by the point of view of the very rich or very powerful.

For example, if your "point of view" is that of a nonwealthy or nonpowerful political group, you might think the taking of hostages is justified. If your point of view is from the perspective of one of the hostages, you might think it not justified at all. If we left the "resolution" at this point, we would not discuss the principle of using people solely as the means to another's end (e.g., taking hostages to wield political power). We would not discuss ways in which a political minority might morally achieve their desired ends. We would not discuss the dilemma of choosing between political expediency and moral obligation.

In failing to consider these various questions and in accepting a relativistic resolution of this type ("It all depends on your point of view"), we allow events in the world "to take their own course," which ultimately permits practices in the world which might well be less just, less moral or less effective than they could be. We seem to be suggesting that ordinary persons, while affected by practices in the world, are somehow not clever enough to decide (and implement) what practices they would rather live with and encourage. In other words, Context Relativism could lead us to think that the rightness of a belief or action is determined by this or that variable of the context, rather than by our evaluation of *what* is believed or of *what* is done (just as the student originally felt that the large class and competition to law school *required* that one cheat, i.e., that the student "had no other choice" if a passing grade was desired).

15. Increasing our Knowledge of the World

When the uniqueness of the context is stressed, the Context Relativist seems to be denying that a knowledge claim bears any relation to any other statement, logical or otherwise (consider the conception of change as radical departure). But surely we wish to depict in our body of knowledge many such connections or relations: logical, physical, causal, social, psychological, historical. In systematizing these relations, we provide a standard or norm which allows us to identify our experiences and endow them with significance. (I learn to recognize and name the experience of feeling sorrow and associate this feeling with the loss of something dear to me.) The presence of a standard or means of classification permits me to unify diverse experiences (so that I understand that the theft of my typewriter and the death of my dog are both losses which will precipitate my feeling sorrow). Similarly, the relations embodied in our knowledge claims are public (since the knowledge claims are themselves objective and universal), so I am able to recognize your response to the loss of something dear to you.

Standards and norms codify, as well, the familiar patterns of our daily life. Presumably the Context Relativist, like the rest of us, wants the bus to be on time or the car to start, expects a familiar environment to remain reasonably stable and predictable, wants others to keep promises and treat people fairly and justly, expects events to be explainable and beliefs to be rational. Most likely the Context Relativist does not intend to deny that there are such regularities and expectations, but the position of Context Relativism leaves us unable to explain the regularities and without means of justifying our expectations.

Norms can be rules of behavior ("Chew your food with your mouth closed"), rules of meaning ("A chair is something you sit on"), conventions ("At a traffic light, you stop for red, go for green"), prescriptions ("Love thy neighbor"), mores ("It is customary to throw rice at weddings—on the married couple"), protocol ("One shakes hands upon being introduced to another person"), rules of grammar ("Adjectives modify nouns, adverbs modify verbs"), casual agreements ("Everyone in the neighborhood will put their grass clippings out only on collection day").

Other kinds of standards appear in definitions, law-like statements, hypotheses or theories. "Planets revolve around the sun," "Steam is actively moving water molecules,"

"2+2=4," "A foot is 12 inches," are all fixed points of reference which enable us to make standard measurements, classify features of the empirical world, compare one aspect of the world with another and to explain the phenomena we observe around us.

Notice that when we appeal to some fixed point of reference, we will say "Event x is relative to definition (theory, point of view) y." For example, "Steam is actively moving water molecules" is a simplistic definition introduced early in our science training. But in order for even such a simplistic definition to be intelligible, we must have a theory in which molecules are identified and their role in the constitution of matter made explicit. In this case, the definition is said to be meaningful relative to molecular theory. Even though molecular theory is but one way of explaining the physical world, the theory must apply universally—to all physical objects. The theory is obliged to describe *every* occurrence of steam, not just that which flows from my teakettle this afternoon. (Hence, the claims made by the theory will be universal.)

When Einstein said that time is relative to the motion of bodies (and popular relativists cheered—mistakenly), he was seeking to explain, universally, variations in our observations and experiences of time. Rather than there being a unique relationship between an individual and a fast train, Einstein offered a theory which explains *every* variation of time (or at least one which explains more than prior theories did). His theory, in other words, sets forth the conditions under which time will "slow down" or "speed up."

When astronomy claims that the rotation of the planets depends on their mass and initial spin which includes the gravitational pull from the sun, such computation is not unique to this planet, this time and this place. Such a claim provides a standard point of reference by which the rotation of any planet in our solar system can be determined and explained. It is in this sense that fixed standards can enable us to increase our knowledge: norms and theories provide standard points of reference by which any of us can guide our investigations. They provide sufficient uniformity and regularity to be able to make signifcant judgments about the world, note variation and seek explanation.

We can let Aristotle summarize our response here to the Context Relativist:

> . . . [T]he fact that a thing is explained with reference to something else does not make it essentially relative.
>
> From this it is plain that, if a man definitely apprehends a relative thing, he will also definitely apprehend that to which it is relative. Indeed this is self-evident: for if a man knows that some particular thing is relative, assuming that we call that a relative in the case of which relation to something is a necessry condition of existence, he knows that also to which it is related. For if he does not know at all that to which it is related, he will not know whether or not it is relative.[13]

It seems, from this, that the Context Relativist has confused relations which can be depicted in universal knowledge claims with a "special" connection between two things (also capable of representation in our knowledge claims, but the appeal to "special," as we saw, led our relativist to "unique and nonreproducible"). To claim a relation between two things, e.g., mother to daughter, is to designate something unique, a distinctive connection. But the connection will apply to *all* cases of this relation. This is what the Context Relativist has ignored.

The relativist has narrowed the sense of "unique" to mean "only of this time and place," hence, nonreproducible. When the relativist says that one thing "depends on" another and is, hence, relative, the relativist does *not* mean that this one thing will always be dependent on the other: this is why truth conditions fluctuate for the relativist, for who knows what this one thing will depend on in another situation, at another time?

If you happen to be a die-hard Context Relativist and are still unconvinced of the importance of standards and norms, or are unconvinced of your own dependence on continuity

---

13. Aristotle *Categories* 8a32–8b4, *op. cit.*, p. 22.

and regularity in your world, consider the following imaginary world. In this world, chairs are capable of independent motion. About half the time you try to seat yourself, the chair remains in the same spot. The other half of the time, you fall on the floor as the chair scoots off (or you are dragged along if you attempt to hold the chair still). Even if this quirk of chairs were the sole oddity of this world, you wouldn't just shrug and say "It depends." I think you can imagine yourself seeking some sort of explanation which will enable you to predict when the chairs will move and when they won't. If you are able to predict when a chair will move, you expect to be able to avoid those embarrassing incidents of crashing to the floor (for example when your arms are full of books or when you've come to class late and don't want to be noticed). In other words, you would not merely accept the random behavior of chairs—you would not, as the Context Relativist suggests, assume that each time the chair moves from under you that it's a unique feature of the circumstances peculiar to this time and this place.

In the instances of abuse cited in Section 14, each instance contains a kernel of this need for norms and regularities (even though the abuses themselves are parodies of such a need). In the first instance, to debate the meaning of key terms in a discussion, as we said, is useful insofar as it removes ambiguity and allows genuine investigation to proceed. What we do, for example, in debating how "justice" is to be defined is to *generate a norm* which we will use throughout the discussion. (Of course in the debate we may want to consider what we *want* such a norm to be. Even here, the issue is not a mere verbal dispute but one of how we want justice to be represented in the world.)

Likewise, to recognize aspects of one's upbringing will turn our attention to possible psychological relationships that may increase our ability to function more effectively. If I recognize that my writing-block is a manifestation of an early prohibition against success (which could be preconsciously acquired from a very moral family or a puritanical social environment), I might be able to direct my attention to that prohibition and have no further "need" of a writing-block. But notice that if I accept the "uniqueness" of *my* writing-block ("That's just the way I am"), as suggested by the Context Relativist, I will neither investigate its origins nor feel it bears any similarity to the writing-blocks of others (so will not inquire into their experiences and observations).

The work of Erik Erikson, for example, seeks to carefully generalize the psychological and social conditions which will give rise to various sorts of personal or individual experience. When such an undertaking is successful, when we understand universal conditions under which a person or a group will do such-and-so, or the conditions under which water will boil or nuclear reactors will malfunction, we increase not only our understanding of the world (and of ourselves in the world), we are able to direct our actions more effectively, i.e., avoid the anxiety surrounding writing, satisfy the demands of a group on strike, make a cup of tea, or evacuate an area near an imminent nuclear melt-down.

In this same way "It all depends on your point of view" does acknowledge the need for a stable point of reference to be able to make knowledge claims. The abuse arose in relativizing the point of reference beyond any usefulness. We do not use points of view to inhibit investigation or to promote contradiction: "It's okay to take hostages if you are part of a nonwealthy, nonpowerful political minority and it's not okay to take hostages if you are a hostage." This doesn't make any sense at all. If, however, we use such divergent points of view to expand our understanding of a problem (or, as Hegel would say, to show us an existing, ongoing situation in the world)—the conditions under which someone might feel justified in taking hostages—we will be in a better position to effect a genuine solution. Just as the proposed "justification" of cheating led us to recognize developing practices and emerging conditions in the educational system, so can adopting this or that perspective on a problem lead us to greater understanding of the relevant variables which give rise to the problem.

In Section 12 we discussed the need to identify the underlying continuity in our experience. In the present section we discussed the role of standards and norms in representing this continuity. Our investigation may not necessarily stop with being able to describe these things. We may want to evaluate the worth of what we see in the world around us. Smith and Jones are talking about the same legal system, one which affects both of them. They don't just accept and describe existing unjust practices but seek to understand how to modify (change) these practices to make sure that our existing legal system comes to adopt fairer practices. This dual role adopted by Smith and Jones (of describing the world in knowledge claims and evaluating what is in the world with an eye to change) is possible with a nonrelativist's account of context, but is unlikely to be seen in a relativist's account of context.

True statements are known when what they claim corresponds to what is, in fact, in the world. What they claim must be satisfied in the world. We are able to increase our knowledge of the world because we are able to formulate the conditions under which a claim will be satisfied. We acquire knowledge of our world—scientific, logical, moral, aesthetic, psychological, sociological, etc.—because the truth conditions of a statement *are* satisfied. Such conditions remain fixed and universal, though our body of knowledge is quite capable of expanding and being modified. In this way, we can know much more than tables and chairs. We can know laws, regularities, relations, probabilities and likelihoods. Variations in our experience are not merely idiosyncracies as suggested by the Context Relativist. Genuine idiosyncracies— the truly nonreproducible features of the context—can neither confirm nor disprove what we claim to know, nor can they direct our attention to underlying uniformities in our world.

I would like to leave you with a little puzzle. The brief answer to a question posed by Mike Wallace, a reporter on the television news show "Sixty Minutes," contains *two* classic appeals to popular Context Relativism. You might enjoy finding them and formulating them more fully. In an interview with Frank Terpil, a former employee of the CIA who currently sells arms to Latin American countries, Lybia and other countries, Mike Wallace asked: "I don't mean to come across as pious, but doesn't the morality of what you do concern you?" Terpil replied, "In today's world, if what you do makes a buck, it's okay. If I didn't do it someone else would."[14]

14. "Sixty Minutes," CBS, aired 8 November 1981.

CHAPTER FOUR
Cultural Relativism

16. The Argument from Language

In Chapter Three we saw the Context Relativist turn from the immediacy of the present to the recognition that the variables of the environment can point to the underlying continuity and uniformities of our world. Similarly, the Naive Relativist in Chapter Two discovered how all-important subjective statements can be used to acquaint us with the larger, more public world of objects, events and issues. In both cases, the relativist was drawn towards something a little beyond this particular situation or that particular feeling. In seeing more than uniqueness in the present, the relativist has (perhaps with some reservation) begun to explore the realm of objectivity and universality in knowledge.

The crux of trying to show objectivity and universality is to figure out how much we can reasonably expect to know (without, of course, merely accepting or resigning ourselves to ignorance). I mean that even with a wealth of technical data, we may not be seeing the world exactly as it is (though if we don't stop to think about it, we expect that the world does exactly resemble our perception of it). In seeking limits to knowledge, then, we do not seek to constrain ourselves, rather we seek to distinguish which of our beliefs are more hypothesis than fact, which of our beliefs are reliable enough to act upon.

Even more important, in trying to show objectivity and universality in knowledge we reveal a basic curiosity about how the world works, how we are affected by it and how we can, in turn, act effectively and creatively. The relativist, I suspect, has no desire to dampen our curiosity nor even claim that the world can't be known (since the relativist is making an effort to explain this world, as well). It is an unfortunate consequence of the various relativistic positions that they ultimately encourage us to turn away from the larger world about which we are so curious.

In this spirit of curiosity, Cultural Relativism appears to offer a plausible means of investigating the world. In claiming that our beliefs and perceptions, values and practices, institutions and even "human nature" are determined by our social environment, the Cultural Relativist seems to turn our attention to the larger world (beyond this situation or my feelings) which is diversely populated by unique cultures. In coming to know other cultures, other practices and beliefs, reasons the Cultural Relativist, we are coming to know the world. Of course knowledge claims won't be universal. But, continues the relativist, given our dependence—intellectual as well as physical—on our society, perhaps we have gone as far as we can in our search for universality.

Consider, the relativist might say, identical behaviors observed in the United States and in France. Two men embrace in public, exchanging a hug and kisses on both cheeks. In the United States an observer might label this an act of homosexuality. In France an observer would label this an act of greeting. Each label is simply reflecting the early training each observer received in acquiring his/her language and social conventions. Don't all our perceptions, beliefs about the world, practices and attitudes simply reflect the conventions of our culture as this example suggests?

When I talk here about conventions, I refer to the conventions of naming things as well as to the conventions of behavior. One of the strongest arguments put forth by a Cultural Relativist appeals directly to our dependence on

language to be able to classify and make any sense out of
our experience in the world. The following argument, which
I am calling the Argument from Language, seeks to demonstrate the extent of this dependence:

1. Knowledge claims are expressed in, and can only be
   expressed in, some language.
2. Our descriptions of the world are limited to the conceptual framework implicit in the language (i.e., the
   concepts we use to identify the things and events around
   us).
3. The conceptual framework itself reflects the unique cultural biases, mores, etc. of that group using the language.
4. In other words, the use and meaning of the concepts
   in this framework are governed by culture-bound conventions.
5. Hence, these cultural meanings must necessarily be included in any statement of truth conditions for a claim.
6. Therefore, the evaluation of a knowledge claim is relative to the culture in which it is made.

Normally when we hear "culture" used in this way we think
of specific racial groups—a Malaysian tribe, Anglo-Saxons—
or of specific national groups—American or Russian society.
But in the above argument "culture" can refer to an historical
period (e.g., the eighteenth century), political groups (e.g.,
the Gray Panthers, the oil lobby), regional identities (hos-
pitable Southerners, taciturn New Englanders)—any group,
in other words, which fundamentally affects the perception
of and practices in the world of its members.

Because the concepts used by a group to be distinctively
recognizable are unique to that group, knowledge is thought
by the relativist not to be universal. I.e., everybody either
consciously or accidentally identifies with a nation, an interest
group, or a recognizable community of some sort ("I am a
good, upstanding American," "I am a feminist," "I belong
to a rock group."). Hence, argues the relativist, we can never
fully extricate ourselves, conceptually, from the influence of
a larger community, and whatever we know (or claim to
know) will really reflect this influence. Whereas the nonrelativist does want knowledge to truly describe the world, the

relativist concludes that at best knowlege claims describe only the beliefs of a culture.

Popular support for the position of Cultural Relativism is largely gathered from the seemingly inexplicable (to us) beliefs and practices of other societies. Navaho culture shares American land with the dominant Anglo-Saxon culture but has little else in common with it. Even a seemingly universal concept such as time is radically different in the two cultures. Our familiar division of minutes, hours, days seems, to us, fairly straightforward and uncomplicated. We can efficiently arrange our activities by this means: "I work from 9 to 5," "Can you meet me at 3?", "Do you have time to take me to the station?" But for a Navaho working in the Anglo culture, such discreet units (minutes, hours) as well as our passion for punctuality and schedules may be totally mysterious and inexplicable. It's not that the Navaho can't understand what the units of time are; it's more that these divisions may seem to him/her arbitrary and fairly pointless.

On the other hand, the Navaho concern with the ancestral past and the treatment of dead relatives as vital and present spirits seems to us equally inexplicable. Even if a Navaho were to patiently explain to us that the continuity of life gives one a moral obligation to care for these spirits, we might think this a quaint, perhaps exotic, line of reasoning but certainly arbitrary and pointless. Our Anglo-derived language contains no words, no means, to convey the compelling duty that the Navaho feels from an ancient past. The depth of the feeling can be seen, though, in the obligation the Navaho automatically takes on for his/her ancestors as well as for future generations.

Examples of this sort abound in anthropological literature. The beliefs of other cultures appear elusive to us for several reasons. Each culture will have a fairly sophisticated set of terms which reflects areas of cultural expertise and interest. The properties of snow, for example, are elaborately categorized and investigated in the Eskimo language and culture. Our own primitive designations of "powder," "icy," "drifts of," "one inch of," "packed" would leave the Eskimo somewhat helpless to carry on. Similarly, the scientific language of our culture which refers to "neutrinos" and "black holes" would be thought utterly frivolous by members of a rain forest tribe. So the differing concerns of cultures can act as a barrier to our recognition and respect for possible insights into the world and make us think that universality in knowledge is an empty ideal.

Likewise, we may fail to appreciate which beliefs are truly dominant in a culture. Such "misreading" was thought to account for the difficulty the United States had in negotiating the release of the hostages in Iran. U.S. negotiators failed to grasp the depth of religious commitment in Iranian culture nor did they recognize the long-seated belief in the authority of the clerics. Hence Western leaders (and this would be true of any unenlightened Western leader) mistakenly addressed their efforts to less powerful government personnel, assuming that the [Western] belief that authority resides with the secular government was universal.

Hence, says the relativist, our ignorance and our quest for universality is a lethal combination, yielding only dangerous misunderstanding and error. Here the relativist's claim is given its strongest formulation: not only *is* knowledge relative (to this or that culture) but it *should* be relative. In this way we will avoid insisting on using our own beliefs or enforcing our own practices when dealing with another culture.

The point of this particular section, though, is not to argue either the merits or the weaknesses of the position, but to make sure that you are clear about the difference between what the relativist wants to claim is knowledge and what the nonrelativist claims. The Cultural Relativist says that knowledge can only be a description of a particular culture or group. The nonrelativist wants knowledge to be a genuine description of the world.

Let's leave, for the moment, exotic examples from anthropology and see how this distinction would be made in the ordinary, everyday world shared by the relativist and the nonrelativist. Let's say that I'm sitting in my chair watching a children's game being played outside the window. The Cultural Relativist will say that this description just reflects the dominant beliefs of my culture rather than genuinely depicting states of the world. Where I—a nonrelativist—might assert that there is, in fact, a chair here and that I am indeed sitting on it, a popular Cultural Relativist would point out that the object on which I am sitting is what we in Western civilization call a "chair" and that the practice of seating ourselves on such objects is also idiosyncratic to Western culture. Other cultures may call such an object something else and may put it to different use.

On the other hand, I as a nonrelativist want to insist that even though other cultures may not utilize chairs nor manufacture them nor even need them since their citizens may sit cross-legged on the ground, the four-legged wooden object with a back and arms on which I sit *is* just that—a four-legged wooden object with a back and arms which supports weight, regardless of who sees it, regardless of who sits on it, regardless of who might want it, regardless of what we might call it or use it for.

Similarly, the relativist might point to the children outside and say that their activity is simply what we in our culture designate as a game, though this same activity might well be seen as something quite different to a resident of sixteenth-century England, where this activity might be seen as truancy from work.

Again, I as a nonrelativist would point out that there are children on the lawn (whom anyone can see), there is a pattern to their activity (which can be identified by an observer, even a relativist), and that this activity reaches some sort of climax at regular intervals. Hence, continues the nonrelativist, all the conditions have been satisfied for showing that a game is in progress. Other cultures (for example, the Hopi tribe) may have a different word for it, but they too will have a concept with these same conditions for an activity engaged in by their children. Even the fact that some cultures or classes may not use such concepts as 'game' or 'play' (for example, in some castes in Pakistan children are the sole means of a family's support, hence they would have little use for these concepts) does not mean that there is no such concept as 'game' or no such activity in the world.

Though the relativist and nonrelativist appear to be actively arguing the two sides, the intent here is simply to represent the two positions so that you have a clear idea of what the two sides of the debate are. Using the Argument from Language, the relativist adopts the strategy of showing how each of our knowledge claims ultimately reflects the values, practices and attitudes of a culture rather than objectively and universally describing the world.

But the nonrelativist wants to insist (and will argue later in the chapter) that we *can* depict states of the world, a world that is, for all intents and purposes, independent of cultural conventions and restrictions; a world that does have chairs, and children's games, and floundering or healthy economies, and obligations to educate; a world that includes individuals having distinct and recognizable goals, needs and aspirations. These objects, activities and desires constitute a world available to all persons of all cultures. The crucial difference then between our relativist and our nonrelativist is this: do our knowledge claims tell us about the world or just about some culture or group?

17. Social Scientists at Work: Benedict and Marx

Very often the Cultural Relativist will appeal to the work of social scientists as conclusive evidence that the Argument from Language succeeds in showing the futility of requiring that knowledge claims be universal. That is, says the relativist, the Argument from Language proves that our very thought is wholly a product of our culture. Since thought (awareness, cognition) is essential in getting to know the world, what we "know" about the world must necessarily embody the beliefs of our culture. Social scientists, continues the relativist, have proven that particular cultural beliefs are not universal (i.e., they are not always held by other cultures). Hence our knowledge claims (e.g., our descriptions of the world) are equally incapable of being universal.

As you will see in Section 21 I will reject the claim that the work of social scientists requires that we all become

Cultural Relativists. But in this rejection I do *not* want to reject the work itself. Our knowledge of the world and our methods of investigation have been deeply enriched by the works of such people as Ruth Benedict (in anthropology) and Karl Marx (in political science as well as philosophy). Hence, it is vitally important to distinguish their work and their role in helping us to overcome many of our prejudices from their seeming support of relativism.

Ruth Benedict used her work in anthropology to show us how much of our behavior arises from the dominant values and expectations of our culture (something we take for granted now). Hence, in investigating any culture we should always seek to present the behavior of people in that culture in the light of the formal structure of that culture (e.g., the institutions of that culture). Her conclusions might appear to us as fairly tame, but at the time they constituted a considerable challenge to both the field of anthropology (where an anthropologist was expected to use the prevailing Victorian standards of the West to "study," judge and evaluate various societies) and the prevailing cultural belief in Anglo supremacy.

Benedict's emphasis on the uniqueness of cultures[1] served to dispel much of the ethnocentrism demonstrated by her contemporaries. ("Ethnocentrism" refers to the belief that one's cultural values are the right ones and that one's perception of the world is the accurate one, hence both are

---

1. Behavior, for example, will take on a distinctive meaning for each society: ". . . each one [behavioral configuration] is an empirical generalization, and probably is not duplicated in its entirety anywhere else in the world." Every behavior, in other words, every action will reflect something unique about the culture, not just about the person performing the action. A person's action gives form to, physically expresses, and draws attention to specific characteristics of the society. No behavior, says Benedict, no matter how trivial, is duplicated (or can be duplicated) meaningfully elsewhere. Schmidt may drink beer out of a riding boot at his fraternity initiation in Austria, but Smith is expected to steal a stop sign for his initiation to a fraternity in the United States. It would be meaningless for Smith to drink beer out of a riding boot. See Ruth Benedict, *Patterns of Culture* (Boston: Houghton-Mifflin, 1959), p. 238.

acceptable standards by which to assess the belief of another culture.) Requiring that field workers learn the native language and concepts, that they seek to describe native practices and rituals as accurately as possible without interpretation, and that they cultivate an attitude of respect for the people they study, enabled anthropology to emerge as a respectable scientific discipline.

Until that time, the prevailing Western belief in the supremacy of Anglo culture crippled investigation. The belief was certainly not confined to anthropology. Missionaries were sent (and still are) by our churches to enlighten people of non-Christian societies and to Christianize practices of those societies judged (by our standards) to be heathen. "An old Indian once told me that when the missionaries arrived they fell on their knees and prayed. Then they got up, fell on the Indians, and preyed."[2] Though souls were "saved" and cultures "studied," numerous nonwhite groups were badly exploited and the integrity of their culture undermined by representatives of Anglo culture. This may not have been particularly intentional or malicious; nonetheless, one's credibility as an objective observer was lost. The value of inaccurate, biased data is nil, not to mention the moral questionability of using others for one's own ends.

Hence, Benedict was able to help curb some forms of exploitation while at the same time provide field workers with valuable tools of investigation. We, too, can benefit from Benedict's teaching. Like her field workers, we, too, do not give much thought to the beliefs we use daily and the things we do. Usually, we take these beliefs and actions for granted. An observer of another culture, of course, can take nothing for granted and certainly must be on guard against biased interpretation. If we use these same tools (i.e., suspending our own beliefs while becoming acquainted with the beliefs and practices of another group), we might, for example, lose the label of the "ugly American" abroad as

2. Vine Deloria, Jr., *Custer Died for Your Sins: An Indian Manifesto* (New York: Avon Books, 1972), p. 105.

well as be more likely to promote sympathetic dialogue between warring ethnic, ideological or political groups at home.

One of the most reliable means of accurately becoming acquainted with the dominant values in a given culture, of learning the "distinctive meaning" of various behaviors, and of coming to know what that society expects of its members is to look at the institutions of that society. The phrase "institutions of a society" refers to the society's public means of caring for its members. The manner in which one is educated, the laws which define acceptable behavior, the dominant or accepted religious practices, are some of society's institutions:

> If we are interested in human behavior, we need first of all to understand the institutions that are provided in any society. For human behavior will take the forms those institutions suggest. . . . [A]ny society selects some segment of the arc of possible human behavior, and in so far as it achieves integration its institutions tend to further the expressions of its selected segment and to inhibit opposite expressions.[3]

Benedict says, in effect, that in order to interpret a person's behavior one needs to look at the dominant mode of social organization: is this an agricultural society, nomadic, industrial? The institutions, then, will cater to the particular goals of the society, e.g., a highly technological society will need to provide appropriate education for its members to be able to use and maintain the technology as well as improve it. Once we understand the institutions of a society, we need to ask: what behavior will promote this type of society and meet its goals? An agricultural society will need people skilled in raising large crops, education will emphasize successful agricultural techniques used in the past, laws will protect the land and crops and may regulate the use of land and the distribution of crops, religion may describe deities as tied to

---

3. Benedict, *Patterns of Culture*, pp. 236, 254.

the sun, the earth, rain, etc., literature might extol the virtues of an agricultural life.

Hence Benedict's point is simply: don't try to interpret an individual's behavior without taking a look at the institutions of the society, for the institutions will provide the means of identifying the significance of the behavior. (This is sound advice to anyone wanting a deeper understanding of his or her own behavior, as well.)

This point was well made in our early history. In the seventeenth century when universities were opening in the colonies, scholarships were provided to the young men of various native tribes. However the "opportunity" was soon ignored by Native Americans. This is explained in the following letter from an elder of one of the tribes:

> . . . But you, who are wise, must know that different Nations have different conceptions of things; and you will therefore not take it amiss, if our Ideas of this kind of Education happen not to be the same with yours. We have had some Experience of it. Several of our young People were formerly brought up at the Colleges of the Northern Provinces; they were instructed in all your Sciences; but, when they came back to us, they were bad Runners, ignorant of every means of living in the woods, unable to bear either Cold or Hunger, knew neither how to build a Cabin, take a deer, or kill an Enemy, spoke our Language imperfectly, were therefore neither fit for Hunters, Warriors, nor Counsellors, they were totally good for nothing. . . . We will take Care of their Education, instruct them in all we know, and make Men of them.[4]

The lesson should be clear. If we wish to genuinely understand and come to know other cultures, we had better understand what these cultures value, what they teach and what duties their members are expected to perform, what

---

4. Frank Muir, *An Irreverent and Thoroughly Incomplete Social History of Almost Everything* (New York: Stein and Day, 1976), p. 77; from *Biography and History of the Indians of North America*, ed. Samuel G. Drake, 2nd ed. (Boston, 1834).

roles they will fill and what contribution they are expected to make. As Benedict points out, this is only possible when we overcome our own Western biases and deepen our understanding of human behavior and the extent to which our actions are socially determined.

Karl Marx, writing in the nineteenth century, made an even stronger claim, perhaps, for social determinism. He believed that our very own personal identities (what we think, hope for, dream about as well as what we do) must be explained within the social framework: "Consciousness is . . . from the very beginning a social product and remains so as long as men exist at all."⁵ Elsewhere he wrote:

> Our desires and pleasures spring from society; we measure them, therefore, by society and not by the objects which serve for their satisfaction. Because they are of a social nature, they are of a relative nature.⁶

In arguing that consciousness is a social product, Marx denies that human nature (and hence human action) is a given, a fixed and unchangeable essence whose growth and development solely follows natural laws (in the way an acorn "naturally" develops into an oak tree). This means, for example, that for Marx, arguments "proving" the weakness of women or the strength of men by appeal to biological necessity do not prove anything at all.

If consciousness is a social product, then our attitudes towards women and men are in some sense chosen (though perhaps not consciously or intentionally): we could, just as well, see men as weak and women as strong; we could, also, make no gender distinction regarding degrees of strength and talk instead about the range of human strengths and weaknesses. But doesn't this prove, says the relativist, that

5. Karl Marx and F. Engels, *The German Ideology* (1846), ed. C. J. Arthur (New York: International Publishers, 1970), p. 51.

6. Karl Marx, "Wage Labour and Capital" (1849; rev. 1891) in *The Marx-Engels Reader*, ed. R.C. Tucker (New York: W.W. Norton & Co., 1972), p. 180.

whatever we think or do is solely determined by our culture? How on earth can there be a choice?

Consider the following "origins" of our attitudes. Laws "protect" women from certain kinds of jobs, e.g., combat, and mandate that men be legally responsible for the entire family unit. Educational practices encourage women and men to pursue "appropriate" professions, e.g., teaching children and nursing for women, and engineering and truck-driving for men, regardless of either's talents, desires or needs. Religion promotes a conception of family as having highly distinct gender roles; unfortunately for men, the paradigm Father is omnipotent, omniscient, in short, perfect. In this case, says Marx (in agreement with Benedict), we are led to a conception of men as strong and women as dependent.

But in recognizing that these practices are *human* products, Marx also turns our attention to the fact that such practices *can* be changed. Laws are not divinely given, they are conceived and implemented by *persons*. Educational practices are adopted or modified according to how *persons* (educators) perceive the needs of society. Religious dogma can be (and has been) modified by *persons* (the Pope, elders of a church) to better meet the spiritual needs of individuals. The attitudes we hold do not develop in the same way as the color of our hair or our height, but are taught and often changed or rejected.

Like Benedict, Marx gives us the means of vastly expanding our knowledge of the world and of human behavior. Rather than resign ourselves to an unchangeable "human condition," both offer methodological insights which help us to further our investigation. We are offered a means of correcting unfair or oppressive situations; we no longer need to shrug our shoulders and say "Well, what can one do . . . ?" in a resigned tone. Certainly these are valuable contributions. So valuable that we must separate these conclusions from the inference that such conclusions must necessarily lead to adopting Cultural Relativism. This latter inference, as I said above, will be treated separately later in this chapter.

18. The Philosopher's Dilemma Returns:
The Problem of Intersubjectivity

What Benedict and Marx *have* proven, though, is that much of our identity—the very personal way we experience, interact with and present ourselves to the world—is acquired from the culture in which we mature. Not only is the influence of language and culture experienced on a very personal level, but the alliances we form in our daily lives contributes to the formation of who we are and what we will become.

A community of persons shares more than a language consisting of rules for syntax and semantics, more even than cultural norms and prescriptions. We share a wide range of beliefs, history, myths, slang, humor, fears, goals, expectations and rituals. Our lives are intimately intertwined with friends, family, co-workers and more casually connected to a larger network of salespeople, teachers, friends of the family. We are aware first of our responses to this community: we want a friend to like us, we rebel against family opinion, we admire the way a certain teacher presents new material.

I am emphasizing here a small but very important point: we are affected daily by the approval, expectations, desires, disapproval of others, in a word, by the responses of those involved in our daily lives. Similarly, we affect others in these same ways: we approve or disapprove of a friend's action, and expect a certain kind of behavior from them. It's almost a cliché to quote John Donne's famous line, "No man is an island," but it can bring us to the awareness of the profound influence and need we have for a social environment. The very necessity of such an environment should not be overlooked or taken lightly.

Once you have a feeling for the importance of the social world, think about the nonrelativist philosopher's desire (in Chapters One and Two) to move from a private, "subjective" world to a public, "objective" world. This desire is similar to our recognition of how important a social world really is to us: we can see more, do more, know more, and generally have a much better time than if we were totally isolated from others. For our philosopher in Chapter Two, s/he also

believes that if we can show that there really is a public
world (not just private experiences or feelings), we can see
more, do more, know more and work towards a better world.

To this end, the nonrelativist philosopher in Chapter Two
sought to show how we might legitimately become acquainted
with a public world through our private, subjective sensations
and beliefs. When I wanted to prove to you that there was
a chair before me, I asked you to reach out and feel the
object before me. I was actually asking you to experience
the sensation of resistance. This sensation of course is totally
private to the person doing the touching, but the very fact
that I can *anticipate* your sensation reveals my belief that
there is something there besides my sensation and yours,
namely, a chair. When you felt the resistence, you might
have exclaimed: "Well, what do you know, there *is* a chair
here!"

In other words, said the nonrelativist philosopher, we share
a similar understanding of and expectation of a "public"
object or event, one that we *both* can experience, discuss and
verify. This shared understanding of sensation and belief
that there is a public world is the core of "intersubjectivity."
The understanding is "between subjects" who, as subjects,
have a wealth of private, subjective experiences (feelings,
sensations, beliefs) which are assumed to be directly related
to and a necessary part of the public world.

Hence, not only do *we* depend upon such intersubjectivity
in our daily interactions with others in the world, the philosopher depends upon such intersubjectivity to show the
very possibility of knowledge. (Remember that the nonrelativist philosopher would like to show that a knowledge
claim is universal, that the truth conditions for a statement
won't change from person to person. Hence, intersubjectivity—agreement within a community of persons—seems a
good means of beginning to demonstrate universality in
knowledge.)

Similarly, the nonrelativist philosopher wanting to show
the universality of "This is a chair" needs to show that *any*
perceiver coming into my office can, *ceteris paribus*, make
the true claim "Here is a chair." In order for the *subjective*

sensations and beliefs of each observer to *lead them to* the claim "This is a chair," they must obviously be able to recognize chairs and know that these distinctive sensations (or appearances) indicate the presence of such an object.

At this point, the Cultural Relativist and the nonrelativist seem to have arrived at the same place: we are, as social beings *and* as knowers, dependent upon shared norms and concepts. They diverge, as we have seen, on the question of whether these norms and concepts can, in any way, tell us about a world independent of culture and tradition. The Cultural Relativist says we have reached the end of what we can know with culture-dependent beliefs. The nonrelativist says we should be able to overcome the limitations of cultural belief and investigate genuine attributes of the world.

One long and influential philosophic tradition completely by-passes intersubjectivity and our dependence on a [culturally reflective] conceptual framework to be able to show universality in knowledge. According to this tradition, when we see an object, we not only perceive its physical properties, but we apprehend its "essence" as well, its important features that make it distinct from something else. Distinguishing a chair from a dog is not merely a matter of learning the conventions of our language. Each chair and each dog is related to every other chair and every other dog by a unique essence, chairness and dogness or the "ideal" chair and the "ideal" dog. This is not just philosophic game-playing; in our own world we often seek to capture the essential features of an idea or object in a phrase or description. In asking "What's the bottom line," we focus on what we take to be the *crucial* (essential) feature of a financial transaction, namely, how much it will cost me. "Winning isn't everything, it's the only thing," said the late Vince Lombardi (head coach of the Green Bay Packers, 1959–69, and of the Washington Redskins, 1969–70) in depicting the spirit (essence) of football.

This brief digression into essences is to show how one philosophic tradition avoids the problem of intersubjectivity altogether. In understanding the essence of something, we grasp something universal about it (that which is common to all chairs, dogs, financial transactions, or football games).

This universality "resides" in the thing itself; it does not depend on the particular language we've learned or the culture in which we live. We are, in effect, in a direct relationship with the [universal] essence of an object (rather than needing to depend on the mediation of language or culture for our understanding of the essence). Our knowledge claim "This is a chair" is then shown to be universal by appeal to the fact that we depict [correctly] the essence of this object in our statement.

This position avoids the problem of intersubjectivity by claiming that universality originates with the object and not from a shared language. But Cultural Relativism has shown that our language and culture *do* influence our understanding of the world. Hence, to appeal to essences (to show universality) not only ignores an important influence on knowledge, but encourages a questionable schism in our conception of the world: there's an ordinary, everyday, culturally influenced world and then there's the real world (of essences).

If we do acknowledge the influence of language and culture on our understanding of the world, we are led back to the problem of intersubjectivity. The nonrelativist philosopher is left to deal with the question: is knowledge capable of transcending (going beyond) the limits of cultural belief? If so, how do we show this?

It won't be enough for a philosopher to capitulate and simply say: "We are taught judgments and their connexions with other judgments."[7] If this is the only response, then certainly the Cultural Relativist is vindicated and further inquiry into knowledge will cease. Also, such a response misses the crucial question of the dilemma: do we agree because the world presents itself to us or do we agree because we are taught the same things? Then, even if common language training and socialization account for some agreement, can we show that this agreement depicts in any way features of and uniformities in the world?

---

7. L. Wittgenstein, *On Certainty*, trans. G. E. M. Anscombe and G. H. von Wright (New York: Harper & Row, 1972), p. 21e.

One means of showing that there is more than just conventional agreement to knowledge is with the aid of "confirmation" and "explanation." These are ways of gathering evidence which should provide independent, acultural grounds for showing that our knowledge claims are about the world (and not just about this or that culture). But as we look at confirmation and explanation in the next section, keep in mind the question of how language—a product of human need, imagination and invention—can be instrumental in knowing the world independent of our cultural framework. Also keep in mind that if we can transcend these limits, we are in a better position to further intercultural exchange and dialogue.

19. Tools of Evidence: Confirmation and Explanation

Intersubjectivity, as we saw above, is essential in any account of knowledge, objective or relative. Our language and our community both exert a formative influence on our beliefs and actions. But we may not want to say that this is the *only* component to belief and action.

The nonrelativist wants to show that no matter who comes into my office—a student, a Hopi visitor, a Martian—"This is a chair" remains a true claim. This presumes, as we have seen, that my diverse visitors share the concepts of "physical object" and "chair," for example, or concepts which are substantially equivalent. Or, in the case of the Martian, we may have to pantomime the function of a chair. But we expect that an embodied Martian can sit in the chair and can learn the concept enabling him/her/it to recognize other chairs, not just this one in my office.

So what we need confirmation and explanation to do is to show that our experience (sitting in the chair), the uniformities observed in the world (that chairs stay where they are placed under normal circumstances) do in fact inform us of things and uniformities in the world. How do the notions of confirmation and explanation provide such "proof"?

Confirmation is a procedure in which we assume the truth
of a statement, hypothesis, or general law and make very
specific predictions about what will happen on the basis of
the statement, hypothesis, or general law. If these predictions
are successful—if they are realized—we take this success to
"confirm" to some degree the reliability of the original statement, hypothesis or law. A simple example can represent
the method used. Assume the truth of "Here is a chair."
Now, let's make some predictions: if I rest my hand here,
I will encounter resistance; if I seat myself, I won't fall on
the floor. Then I put my hand here and encounter resistance.
I seat myself and I don't fall on the floor. This little test,
which shows my predictions to be accurate, is not fool-proof
in showing there to be a chair here, i.e., the success of my
predictions cannot *guarantee* that my belief that there is a
chair here (for there may be other statements which can
yield the same predictions). However, the success of my
predictions does give me some assurance that my belief is
sufficiently sound to act on. I can feel reasonably safe seating
myself on objects of this sort and will not have to repeat,
each time, my little confirmation test.

Even if my culture chose to insist that I would fall on the
floor when I sat down, I wouldn't. Even if my culture, for
whatever reason, insisted that my feeling resistence when I
put my hand here is fantasy, I would still feel resistance
and so would *anybody else*. In using these examples I do not
intend to be obtuse (and refuse to see the point of relativism)
nor do I intend to say that Cultural Relativism would make
any such claim as "You'll fall on the floor if you attempt
to seat yourself on a chair." I do intend, however, to overstate
the case in these fanciful examples to make the point very
clear.

So long as Cultural Relativism stops the investigation of
knowledge with intersubjectivity—agreement within a community— and claims, as well, that this agreement is *idiosyncratic to this culture or that, all scientific claims* (in whatever
culture) *become indistinguishable from perceptual claims, mythical beliefs or dogmatic claims*. In abandoning the inquiry into
the "nature of" the world beyond convention and culture,

we accept (whether we want to or intend to) prejudice, ill-founded generalizations and transistory fads on a par with carefully investigated claims and well-argued conclusions. This is an exeptionally strong charge I am leveling against popular Cultural Relativism but recall the relativist's claims from Sections 16 and 18 above: (1) Cultural belief is so integrated into our thinking and is so deeply enforced in our daily lives that investigation "outside" of cultural influence is impossible. (Even the work of Benedict and Marx discussed in Section 17 seems to support this claim.) (2) Any demonstration of knowledge must arrive at intersubjectivity. Such agreement is a product of human communities, human "choice." Given the diversity of belief across cultures, there is no reason to assume that agreement "originates" from a world independent of culture.

(1) and (2) are themselves strong statements from the relativist, and do sound plausible if we don't think of what they commit us to. Hence, my fanciful examples on the previous page are intended to be extreme, showing that if we apply (1) and (2) to all knowledge claims, we arrive at a very peculiar position. Its very oddity, I hope, will cause us to stop and think more carefully about what Cultural Relativism would have us give up.

One thing we must give up if we adopt relativism is the use of confirmation as an "independent" means of gathering evidence for our knowledge claims. When truth and "reality" are made relative to a culture, the best that confirmation can show is that the predictions are *consistent* with other cultural belief and, if successful, the predictions can only "confirm" this consistency. For example, the relativist would say that the fact that I don't fall on the floor when I seat myself can only show that the prediction "I won't fall on the floor" is consistent and compatible with other beliefs of my culture, e.g., the belief that there are distinct, rigid physical objects that support weight. Under relativism, any belief (such as the belief that there are physical objects) is accepted, thought true, if it is consistent with the existing body of beliefs in a given culture. It will not be accepted or rejected on the grounds that, in this case, there are (or are not) such objects in the world.

My objection to this trivialization (by the relativist) of the use of confirmation is even more clear when we consider what happens to the use of explanation, our nonrelativist's second tool of evidence. Thus far, confirmation has given us a means of predicting events: "Where there's lightning, there's thunder" enables us to [successfully] predict hearing a clap of thunder after we've seen a flash of lightning. And, sure enough, during the next storm claps of thunder follow flashes of lightning with unceasing regularity.

However, confirmation can't account for these successes: why does thunder always follow lightning? We look now for an *explanation*. In this case we turn to an expert who tells us that lightning and thunder actually occur simultaneously. But sound waves don't travel as rapidly as light waves so we will see the lightning before we hear the thunder. The lapse of time between the two can, additionally, tell us how far away the lightning is from us. (And our expert may continue by showing us how to compute this distance.)

Explanation, then, gives us reasons why, for example, thunder is seen as following lightning. The explanation offers us a clue to the relationship between the perceived phenomena, and may formulate a general law which might account for the relationship. If we were to be very curious about thunder and lightning, having just heard that they occur simultaneously, we might want to find out what atmospheric conditions will produce thunder and lightning. (Notice that this increase in knowledge increased our capacity for prediction, for now we can predict when lightning might occur as well.) We might also investigate wave theory, learning how to compute the speed of light waves and sound waves as well as discovering additional explanations as to why wave theory explains more about our world than other theories.

You can see even in this brief example that confirmation and explanation create an intricate, complex network of ideas, concepts, hypotheses, predictions and built-in checks on the worth of these ideas, concepts and hypotheses. But something else appears as well. Notice as I make predictions successfully, my curiosity about the world is piqued. That is, I am not satisfied just to be "right" about what will happen. I want to know why I am right. So I was prompted to seek an explanation of why my prediction was right. Once I got a reasonable explanation, my interest did not cease: (a) now I am becoming acquainted with previously unknown (to me) areas of the world, (b) thus my curiosity is aroused about these particular areas, and (c) the explanation itself suggests, implicitly, ways of continuing my investigation and increasing my knowledge of the world. In other words, no matter how satisfying an explanation is, a good explanation will prompt further interest and be able to stimulate further investigation.

Let's consider, now, a radically different explanation that is popular in culture X. Culture X is diametrically opposed to ours in describing natural events in terms of the attributes and behavior of God instead of in terms of the laws of science: "Whenever lightning flashes, God is rudely awakened, and the thunder you hear is the roar of His disapproval." For Smithe, a member of culture X, this is a plausible-sounding explanation since there have been times when she herself has roared with disapproval upon being rudely awakened.

Given the presuppositions of culture X, will the notions of confirmation and explanation provide the same benefits for Smithe as they do for Smith in our culture? Smithe is certainly able to make successful predictions, for she does hear thunder after seeing a flash of lightning. Hence the explanation that God is roaring His disapproval seems to be confirmed by her continued successful predictions.

However, Smithe may not find her interest aroused or further investigation encouraged: (a) she doesn't feel new areas of the world are opened up—she's heard the list of God's attributes and behaviors for as long as she can recall; (b) her curiosity, rather than being stimulated, begins to wane, as a result; but (c) being adventurous she decides she does want to pursue this explanation further. Where, then, shall she turn to investigate? She might read more theology, she might critically assess the value of arguments in favor of God's existence and attributes, or she might simply seek to renew her faith, confusing curiosity with heretical doubt.

Our Cultural Relativist, at this point, must be nodding his/her head in approval. Yes, this is the extent of what we can claim for confirmation and explanation. Confirmation shows a statement/prediction/hypothesis to be consistent with other beliefs in the culture. Explanation provides the best account *within* the scope of cultural belief. How on earth is Smithe going to conceive of explanations utilizing concepts she doesn't even possess? Our supposed "benefits," the relativist would say, would be meaningless to Smithe.

But, of course, I want to object to this pessimistic view of human ability. I want to argue, as well, that we give up far too much in thinking confirmation and explanation are solely manifestations of culture. I believe we should allow the two explanations to compete, vie for the status of which is the most adequate or best. I do not want to agree here with the relativist who is bound to say they are *both* right, *both* adequate for their respective cultures. Nor do I want to insist that the first explanation from our Western scientific community is *necessarily* the best explanation, that our beliefs and practices are *always* preferable to those of another culture. I don't think they always are. (And I also think Benedict and Marx showed that without a doubt ethnocentrism is groundless and inhibits the pursuit of knowledge.)

Hence, for any comparison to take place (following Benedict and Marx), we must avoid *prima facie* judgments about the ultimate worth of each explanation, such as "Well it's just silly to think that God roars, so whatever explanation is left must be right." *First*, if you recall, we need to make sure that we understand the opposing conception—not just what it reports but what it means, the role it plays in culture X. Notice that as we genuinely bring ourselves to understand this explanation in culture X and as Smithe acquaints herself with wave theory and the concept of natural law, already all of us have broadened the range of concepts we can appeal to. Already, before we even think about drawing conclusions about the explanations, our perception of the world has acquired a new texture, a new dimension as it were, by acquainting ourselves with how the world appears to members of culture X. This in itself is no trivial achievement.

At this point, the much more difficult question appears. Are there compelling reasons to think that one explanation can be chosen over the other? Can Smithe and I, for example, decide what criterion we should use to judge the competing explanations? I, of course, can jump in with several helpful (i.e., Western) suggestions: Are the explanations logically sound or do they lead to contradictions? Do the explanations offer empirical and public means of verification?

Smithe might, as well, offer additional helpful suggestions: Do the explanations increase our understanding of the nature of God? Do they promote faith or undermine it? This does look like an impasse, but I don't think it has to be. Let's acknowledge Smithe's desire to uphold God's prominent role in her conceptual framework. Even in our culture many thinkers believe that God should be more visibly represented in our daily lives and thoughts. But I am thinking of introducing Smithe to the writing of Newton, for he articulates very vividly the conflict he experienced in holding dear his religious commitment while being irresistably drawn to secular scientific investigation. This, from our culture, comes the closest, so far as I know, to representing the dilemma that Smithe might face.

Smithe on the other hand, might wonder if "Logic" were a Western equivalent to "God." Upon learning they are not equivalent, she might ask, then, why I put so much faith in Logic. Well, I might reply, it's not faith but rationality. (But I might also stop and think: Why is it better for statements to be consistent and coherent than not? What can coherence show us about the world?) Notice that neither Smithe nor I have asked the other to abandon cultural values outright; but we have asked each other to critically extend ourselves beyond the mere acceptance of cultural beliefs.

Already, here, we have begun marking out an area of intercultural exchange. As we proceed it's quite likely that Smithe and I share a curiosity about how the world "really" is, or share a curiosity about which of our respective cultural beliefs might enable us to glimpse a world beyond our culture. She may be exhilerated as she acquires the skills of scientific investigation and I may find my life enriched as I acquire nonscientific skills of acceptance and trust.

But where does this leave us regarding our competing explanations? By now Smithe and I most likely can easily compare (1) which beliefs generate the greatest number of correct predictions, (2) which explanation seems to be most culturally neutral, (3) what mode of inquiry might accomplish our ends most appropriately (for we are both curious about the world we live in). And this comparison can yield a preference for one explanation over the other, *without* our needing to stubbornly and dogmatically cite the authority of our cultural biases.

To be sure, I am presenting a very hypothetical exchange and am asking you to suspend some of your beliefs momentarily. But two features of this exchange seem to point to our continuing the search for objectivity and universality in knowledge. The first is the possibility of extending ourselves, conceptually and intellectually, beyond our immediate cultural beliefs. As Marx showed, we do not have to be bound forever by what we have inherited.

The second, more tacit, import of the above exchange comes clear when we think about what we can lose in allowing relativism to trivialize our notions of confirmation and explanation. However, the exchange between Smithe and me clearly permits strong cultural influences in our thoughts and values; yet as we create a common ground of discourse and as we turn our attention to the possibility of knowing the world beyond our cultural conventions, we are still able to make *significant* use of confirmation and explanation (until we come up with something better).

I am suggesting, of course, that what we gain in seeking to (realistically) preserve objectivity and universality in knowledge far outweighs the "gains" of adopting Cultural Relativism. The tolerance so often associated with relativism appears here more like apathy (the suppression of curiosity), whereas genuine investigation (such as that advocated by Benedict and Marx) seems, perhaps surprisingly, to promote our appreciation of differences without abandoning the gains we have made in our quest for knowledge.

20. Pseudo-Generalization/Pseudo-Knowledge: Abuses

The gains, then, that we have made in our quest for knowledge consist largely in making generalizations, whether in the form of laws, theories, definitions, principles or more tentative statements unifying particular characteristics or events. The whole point of making a generalization is, of course, to posit some underlying relationship between individuals. So, for example, individual chairs can be "united," subsumed, under a single definition of "chair." Last night's occurrence of thunder and lightning can be "united" with all other occurrences of thunder and lightning in a law which tells when lightning and thunder will occur.

The paradigm of generalization is found in the physical sciences with the formulation of "laws of nature." These are said to be universal because they apply equally to all things in nature, i.e., they will be true in every case. For example, every [dense] object, left unsupported, will fall to the ground due to gravitational pull. This "law of gravity" will hold true of bananas and coconuts falling to the ground in tropical regions as well as of a piece of rock or ice tumbling down a snowy slope creating an avalanche in northern regions. It was true when Richard III fell off his horse as a child learning to ride. It will be true when your grandchildren tumble to the ground when they lose their footing.

The law-like statements formulated in the social sciences strive towards the certainty or universality of laws of nature. In making generalizations about the behavior of the economy or the behavior of persons, social scientists point out that these law-like statements can only generate "probable" predictions, what is *likely* to occur. However, their investigation is guided by the desire to formulate principles which have the force and accuracy of laws of nature. (B.F. Skinner believes that he *has* formulated universal laws of human behavior. He argues that his principles of operant conditioning *can* predict human behavior in every case under varying conditions.[8])

The paradigm provided by the laws of nature is also used as we formulate civil laws for regulating society and moral laws to govern human conscience. These laws are primarily normative or prescriptive: they tell us what we should do. As principles "governing" action they resemble laws of nature, which describe the natural forces governing physical substance. But the authority of civil and moral law, of course, is not as powerful or compelling as the authority of laws of nature. The governed objects—people—are not so easily manipulated nor can they blindly obey.

Nonetheless, civil law and moral law consist of generalizations which are intended to be universal: civil law imposes specific obligations on every member of society, as does moral law. Judges, religious leaders and philosophers, for the most part, conceive of these laws as potentially universal and strive to give them the compelling authority inherent in laws of nature. Civil law is thought to derive some authority or effectiveness from the punitive measures used on offenders. Moral law is sometimes thought to derive its authority from God or some divine being.

But particularly in the case of civil law, we don't expect to reach the compelling force displayed by laws of nature— however hard we may try. Civil laws are formulated by legislators, based on their conception of how society should be run; thus they (the laws) are created from human wisdom and ignorance, human altruism and greed. They may be only as just as their creators. Hence, given the inherent "weaknesses" of civil law along with the fact that humans are not so predictable as molecules, gases and waves, the generalizations posited in our legal system are fairly transitory, requiring frequent revision and review.

The examples I am going to use in this section are generalizations which either we accept or are currently accepted

---

8. Cf. Skinner's *Walden II* (New York: Macmillan, 1948) and *Beyond Freedom and Dignity* (New York: Alfred A. Knops, 1971).

by people around us. Because they are generalizations, they resemble to some extent laws and definitions. Sometimes just this resemblance is enough to make them seem plausible (and authoritative); other times we may, like the scientist, seek evidence to support or disprove them. We are also seeing in this chapter that the popular position of Cultural Relativism may not enable us to distinguish between worthy and unworthy generalizations: they are *all* treated simply as descriptions of cultural belief. At this point we are on dangerous terrain: not only do we often make use of unexamined generalizations, but in this chapter we hear the relativist saying that these generalizations have *authority* simply because they *do* depict beliefs of our culture.

"If there's a will, there's a way" conveys the belief that if you apply yourself and work very hard, you can achieve *anything* you desire. It resembles a law in offering universal conditions for achievement and success. It may be used as a basis for inference, like laws, from observed to unobserved states: "Jones lost his job, so he must not have wanted it very badly." We might think that we "know" why Jones lost his job; his loss is "explained" in the above law-like statement.

A Cultural Relativist will say, yes we do believe this and such a belief will motivate people to work hard. It is consistent with other cultural beliefs we espouse, namely, that working hard will earn us a place in heaven (the original belief behind our "work ethic"[9]), that hard work can surmount financial or physical constraints (as evidenced in many "rags-to-riches" stories), that idleness causes want and deprivation (consider the story of the grasshopper and the ant). Hence, this generalization accurately reflects certain beliefs of our culture, concludes the relativist, just as "If there's lightning, there's thunder" conforms to other beliefs of our culture.

In treating these two generalizations as manifestations of cultural belief, the relativist, on the one hand, trivializes the

---

9. This is not to be confused with the "Protestant ethic" coined by Max Weber, the Calvinist belief that if you are successful in your work, you must be one of God's elect.

scientific authority of "If there's lightning, there's thunder" and, on the other hand, elevates the seeming authority of "If there's a will, there's a way." Not only is "If there's a will, there's a way" *false*, as we will see, but it supports highly discriminatory practices and opportunities in education and business and, as a result, actively works *against* correcting such practices.

"If there's a will, there's a way" presupposes that the means for achievement are universally available to everyone, so that success will depend merely on the exercise of one's will. We forget, then, to ask whether the means for achievement *are* available to everyone. As it happens, unfortunately, they aren't. Will power cannot provide universal access to good education (particularly as fees and tuition rise rapidly). Will power cannot provide a job market willing to admit nonwhites and women to high-paying, high-prestige positions nor can will power eliminate long-standing prejudices against these groups.

To be sure, stories abound about *individuals* who overcame poverty and acquired education (Abraham Lincoln), who overcame prejudice against blacks (Thurgood Marshall) and against women (Golda Meier) and who achieved prominence and influential positions. We say that such individuals have "pulled themselves up by their bootstraps" and that this proves that anything can be achieved by will and perseverance. Much can be achieved in this way, to be sure. But these stories don't refer to the many people who helped Lincoln, to Marshall's bits of luck, or to the personal cost Meier may have had to pay for her success.

These stories, as many as there are, show only that a handful of people were lucky enough to make it beyond their circumstances. The circumstances themselves have not changed. For every Abraham Lincoln, there are a million others who cannot manage tuition, whose skills and imagination are likewise impoverished by the social circumstances so that education does not appear as a possibility. For every Thurgood Marshall, there are a million nonwhites victimized by the job market (e.g., earning below minimum wage if they are able to work at all) or excluded from the possibility of "meaningful" careers. For every Golda Meier and Indira Ghandi, there are a million powerless women in every culture.

Without education, without opportunity, without some power, without adequate subsistence, working hard and perseverence cannot insure the "good life." Restricted access to education, limited opportunity and discrimination are *social* problems—though they also create severe personal problems for many individuals. As social problems, our attention—rather than focusing on how lazy some people are—must be on reclaiming the right to a good education *for all*, insuring that opportunity is available *to all*, that power is not a privilege of wealth. It's really silly to say: "Old Mrs. Jones down the street is starving, she must not want to eat very badly." Old Mrs. Jones is brilliantly managing to pay rising rent and fuel bills on a fixed income; at some point this won't be possible no matter how badly she may want to.

Cultural Relativism, in collapsing the distinction between scientific claims and cultural belief, paves the way for this sort of abuse. I certainly am not suggesting that relativists are themselves unsympathetic. But the position of Cultural Relativism, as we are seeing, can lead us to uncritical acceptance of counterproductive as well as false generalizations.

Cultural Relativism also leads to the acceptance of false defintions, a similar though distinct abuse of our language. Definitions, too, are generalizations but in this case the abuse is in uncritically accepting a (false) definition, then using it to formulate beliefs about the things defined; for example, in our history blacks were defined as less intelligent than other races, hence laws restricting their rights were implemented "for their own good" and "to protect their interests."

Normally, in our language, definitions characterize the essential features of a thing—the form and function of a chair, for example, rather than its color or style. They apply to all cases: "Steam is actively moving water molecules" identifies *all* cases of steam, not just the steam from my radiator, teakettle or bathtub. A definition has authority simply because it gives us the means of telling one kind of thing from another. Though we may argue that chairs may or may not have backs, we do this to insure that our definition will include all types of chairs. We don't argue with the premise that the role of a definition is to give us the means of discriminating one kind of thing from another.

Under relativism, the concept of "definition" is weakened in much the same way as were law-like statements. Again, definitions will reflect cultural conventions rather than any "natural" division of kinds of things in the world. This, of course, is the point of the Argument from Language in Section 16.

It might seem that we have overcome abusive use of definitions in rejecting the use of stereotypes to characterize groups of people. To be sure we may be less inclined to say "Blacks are . . . ," "Women are . . . ," "Jews are . . . ," "Poles are . . . ," filling in the blanks with any number of derogatory adjectives: "stupid," "lazy," "irresponsible." We know now that these adjectives do not describe the essential features of a particular group, that they merely reflect a popular prejudice. However, the following examples commit the same error in accepting a popular prejudice as an authoritative definition and then appealing to these definitions as evidence for our beliefs and practices.

The three examples are: "Handicapped persons are not like [are less than] the rest of us," "Homosexuality is a disease," and "Aggression is part of human nature." When we, for example, define persons as "handicapped," we are saying they are impaired, necessarily helpless (in not having full use of their faculties), and hence dependent. We use the category of "handicapped"—"having a disadvantage that makes achievement unusually difficult," according to a dictionary—to separate and exclude only those persons with *apparent* physical or mental restriction. (If we don't "see" any restriction, we take a person to be normal and treat them as such until we learn differently.) The definition says they are disadvantaged, so, we reason, we should feel sorry for them, expect less of them.

Once we place such persons in a category associated with *dependence*, usually reserved for young children, we expect them to behave much like children; indeed, we see them much as we see children, as unformed and incomplete persons. We treat them sometimes as we would children—with condescension and dismissal—and we assume that they live in a diminished world. This extreme bias towards persons with apparent physical or mental restrictions is cultivated in the way we conduct telethons to raise funds for the treatment and research of various diseases. The paradigm telethon is Jerry Lewis's on behalf of muscular dystrophy. Even though adults may suffer from this malady, the mode used to raise money is emotional, focusing on very small, very attractive children, and stressing their *helplessness* and *dependence* on our generosity.

Hence a range of cultural belief and practices together support (confirm) the definition of apparently restricted persons being disadvantaged, outside the range of "normal" interests and expectations for achievement. Since this is a separate group, construction planning, for example, rarely includes ramps and wide doors at entrances, restaurants will not think to leave aisles wide enough for wheelchairs or crutches. These are subtle ways of reinforcing the exclusion from our world that is anticipated in the definition.

When we define homosexuality as a disease, we place it in the category of pathology—unhealthy, sick, abnormal. This, as does any definition, provides a *starting point* of further inquiry and prediction. Our inquiry, then, will most likely focus on diagnosis and treatment to "cure." We will investigate the antecedent conditions giving rise to the "disease," and will carefully delineate manifestations or symptoms to aid in diagnosis.

From such a definition, our predictions about the behavior of [self-proclaimed] homosexuals will not fall within the range of our expectations for "normal" human behavior, but will be relegated to a special class of "infected" people not fully responsible for their behavior. Metaphorically we put on glasses tinted with our expectations for the abnormal and look at the behavior of these individuals to see in what way it's abnormal. (This "enlightened" view is currently being challenged by the older view that homosexuals are emissaries of the devil, the position taken by Anita Bryant, head of Protect Our Children, Inc., an organization instrumental in the passage of anti-homosexual legislation, Dade County, Florida, 1977–78. You might want to see what this category would generate in terms of investigation and prediction.)

When we define aggression as intrinsic to human nature, we assume it to be a given, unchangeable, necessary part of our behavior. Our tolerance of rape, child and spouse abuse, war, particularly combative sports, dog fighting or cock fighting, mass slaughtering of animals who also share our world all "confirm" the seeming inevitability of human aggression. Nor are we held wholly responsible for our acts of aggression; when seen as instinct, aggression towards others is thought to be an "unfortunate" but excusable offense.

What, then, does this definition lead us to expect from human behavior. Predicting outbursts of aggression will be fairly difficult for we assume that people will try to hold their feelings in check. Hence, acts of aggression will be fairly random, occurring when the person can no longer contain the aggressive feeling: "I was just so angry I couldn't help myself," "I didn't want to keep hitting her, I just couldn't stop myself." If we can't predict aggressive acts accurately, at least we expect them to appear once in a while in every area of human behavior. But this random character, along with our belief that humans are at bottom aggressive, certainly doesn't promote trust and confidence in our fellow beings. When we are not held fully responsible for our aggressive behavior, we will have no recourse but to be a resigned victim or aggressive victimizer—hardly the healthiest state for social relations.

But, you may say, this *is* what aggression is, what homosexuality is, what a handicapped person is. They may not be pleasant facts, but they are facts nonetheless. I, on the other hand, am suggesting the only reason these "facts" seem so obvious is because this is how our culture defines these behaviors and characteristics. From the definitions, supporting beliefs and practices are generated which then seem to turn around and support (confirm) the original definition. This is exactly the position Cultural Relativism must take, for "definition" becomes, as we saw, "cultural designation of objects and attributes."

But such a view of definition *corrupts* our concepts of personhood, of sexual expression and of responsiblity, as we have seen in the above three examples. Such a view of definition (as authoritative categories of a culture) *misuses* our critical abilities and undermines our search for sound moral guidelines, for morality will also have to become a manifestation of culture rather than a search for the universal conditions of "good" and "right." And, of course, the persons unfortunate enough to be included in the categories discussed in our examples suffer from being the recipients of our prejudices.

In saying that we have corrupted our concepts of person, of sexual expression and of responsibility, I am suggesting that all these concepts have been narrowed by these cultural definitions and have thus lost their function, which is to offer the essential characteristics of a thing. When someone having *superficial*—surface, immediately visible—physical or mental restrictions (easily identified by the use of a wheelchair or attendant) is relegated to a special category of "disabled person," our concept of "able person" becomes "one who is superficially unblemished." This is a severe narrowing of the related concept "normal person" as "a human being distinct in the ability to freely choose and act, to create and modify the world around them, to become a fully responsible and self-determining agent." The superficial differences, then, are *accidental*, not essential, characteristics. Just as we construct doors seven feet high to accommodate persons over six feet tall, so are we able to construct ramps to accommodate persons using wheelchairs as their means of locomotion.

Just as we want our definition of chairs to include only the essential features of *all* chairs, so do we want our definition of persons to include only the essential features of *all* persons. Notice that the expanded definition eliminates any justification for treating human adults as children, eliminates resentment for the "burden" of adding ramps to buildings as well as resentment caused by the "inconvenience" of assisting a person through a doorway. (We "normal" persons *expect* our shortcomings and limitations to be respected: "I can't fly, you know we'll have to drive," "I'm just no good at math; you pay the bills," "I'm grumpy in the morning; wait until I've had my coffee to talk to me." In fact we feel justified in flying into a rage should someone forget our "special needs.") We will, at the other extreme, eliminate the tendency to gush and fawn over the normal tasks performed by superficially resricted persons.

Likewise, we narrow our conception of human sexuality in claiming that homosexuality is a disease. If it is a disease, then the cure is heterosexuality and all will be well. We forget, however, that many heterosexual practices are not necessarily exemplary of intimate exchange: sado-masochism, excessive fixations and ritual, bondage, as well as the frequency of frigidity, impotence, absence of affection and trust together belie our conception of heterosexuality as the epitome of sexual expression. Perhaps existing definitions of human sexuality are inadequate and themselves need re-examination. Cultural Relativism, however, cannot lead us to such re-examination or critical rejection of our current definitions, for relativism judges a definition solely by the extent to which it captures cultural belief. And surely these definitions are "accurate," given our beliefs, prejudices and practices. In failing to investigate a more adequate conception of human sexuality, we condemn ourselves to a range of narrow and unresponsive behavior.

Similarly, "Aggression is part of human nature" narrows our current conception of responsibility, namely, that we are "liable and accountable for our actions, the consequences of our actions and the obligations we incur." If I hit your dog with my car, I am obliged to take it to the vet, inform you, and take on the financial obligations of returning your pet to health. If I promise to water your plants during your absence, I will do just that. Both you and I know and agree on the extent of my obligation and *you depend on* (and can reasonably expect) me to fulfill my part of the agreement. This concept of responsibility clearly enables us to live harmoniously and cooperatively.

When we narrow our defintion of responsibility to eliminate whatever acts are "compelled by instinct," the extent to which I can depend on our agreement is weakened (for, you will recall, aggressive outbursts are not predictable). Who knows when you will be overwhelmed by aggressive instinct? At the same time we say we abhor violence—we are appalled by the frequent incidence of muggings, the death of a bystander at a violent confrontation, the injuries sustained by hostages or victims of harrassment. And yet, so long as we accept and maintain a narrow conception of responsibility, we tacitly condone such violence (in offering the possible excuse "I just couldn't help myself.")

On the whole, cultural belief—whether depicted in law-like statements, definitions or general associations—appears unreliable as a basis of knowledge. The weakness of cultural belief is further evidenced in the fact that many of our popular generalizations blatantly contradict one another: "Money is the root of all evil," and "Poverty is a sure sign of laziness"; "The President will do what's best for the country," and "Politicians are not to be trusted," to cite but two examples. How then can any of these beliefs generate knowledge? Though the relativist will not want to support any of these abuses, the position of relativism offers no means of distinguishing justified belief from mere prejudice—all, to the relativist, are manifestations of culture.

But when we *need* generalizations to guide our investigations of the world and of people in the world, surely we must be able to select which of the generalizations are *worthy of* investigation:

> Laws provide a framework for events which we use as a convenient grid for plotting phenomena that may need explanation. ... Their importance lies not in the *precision* with which they trace the characteristics of events or substances but in the fact that they provide a readily identifiable pattern. ... They often serve as the *starting point* from which we survey the events ... not only as the *rules under which we try to bring them*.[10]

---

10. Michael Scriven, "Explanations, Predictions, and Laws" in *Readings in the Philosophy of Science*, ed. B. Brody (Englewood Cliffs, N.J.: Prentice-Hall, 1970), p. 101.

Where the starting point is itself biased, investigation will
be biased. Where the starting point leads to contradiction,
the investigation can only reach an impasse. Where prejudice
is assumed, the investigation can only confirm the prejudice
or reach a dead-end. Where generalizations are ill-founded
and insubstantial, so will knowledge be as well.

21. Science and Knowledge

Given the work of Benedict, Marx and other social scientists, however, we see that the influence of language and
culture must be considered in our account of knowledge.
Given the abuses described in the last section, we might feel
avoiding such abuses justifies minimizing the role of language
and culture. (In other words, we are led to the inference
described in Section 17 above: that since language is reflective
of a culture and since the beliefs of a culture are not universal,
descriptions we offer of the world in knowledge claims must
be nonuniversal and meaningful only for the culture in which
they occur. It might seem that if we want to avoid this line
of reasoning to avoid the abuses, then we must ignore the
substance of Benedict's and Marx's work.)

"Because [our desires and pleasures] are of a social nature,"
said Marx in Section 17 above, "they are of a relative nature."
We could, superficially reject the problem facing us with the
Aristotelian response from Chapter Three: if you know that
to which a thing is relative, then you know something about
that thing that will not change; an essential feature of a
thing may well be its relation to something else, as a daughter
to her mother. Hence, to say that consciousness is a social
product tells us that *all* human minds are dependent in
distinct and identifiable ways on the culture in which they
mature.

But if we only say to Marx (and the others) "You can't
possibly be a relativist, for your conclusions about human
identity and behavior are universally applicable, your recommendations for investigation universally valid," we fail to
address the more difficult issue of how to achieve knowledge

which is objective and universal when we are so deeply dependent for this knowledge on cultural beliefs and conventions. Our exchange with Smithe from culture X in Section 19 above suggests that we can transcend the limitations of culture. But the exchange doesn't show how this might be done, nor does it show how our language—limited though it may be—itself can *enable* us to achieve a certain conceptual independence.

Hence at this point we should think of how intersubjectivity can, or might be able to, get us to universality and what features of language, any language, might permit such a move. The obvious points about language include: (1) language is acquired by instruction and imitation; we are taught to uniformly identify a particular stimulus with a particular response; (2) no matter what the language is, every language at some point enables the user to be a "self-teacher," that is, one is able to correct him/herself, acquire new concepts and analyze old concepts without instruction, and evaluate the concepts and conventions used; (3) evaluating the use of the language leads one to a recognition of the formal structure of his/her language and the possibility of understanding the necessary structure of every language.

Two brief conclusions will suggest how we might begin responding to the problem of achieving universal knowledge of an objective world in the face of cultural limitation. Notice that the language we are taught (whatever the language) is public and describes a public world, one shared by the speakers of the language. That the language is public and our instruction the same as others in our community guarantees intersubjective agreement, at least within this community. Since the language is public and can be acquired by instruction, we can conclude that *any* person is capable of acquiring it. Here, then, we see a possible road from intersubjectivity to universality: intersubjective agreement is guaranteed in any language since each person is using the same concepts to identify the same sorts of things in the world; a nonnative to our language, as Benedict shows us, is perfectly capable of acquiring our language *and* access to our culture, though his/her own language and culture may be radically different.

This capacity suggests, then, how humans can transcend cultural limitation. Not only can we come to know other "conceptual frameworks," but we see evidence in our own culture of being able to *create* such frameworks beyond the limitations of our ordinary, everyday language. The abstract languages of physics, biology and computer technology, and the language of thought, feeling and sensation exemplify this ability.[11] We can talk to each other of chairs having seats and being capable of supporting weight. But to explain why this is so, to investigate the properties of chairs in any depth, we need concepts more sophisticated than those of our ordinary, everyday language. We need to enter (or construct) the conceptual framework of atomic or molecular theory to investigate the physical properties of objects. If I want to know how I come to know the physical properties of objects, we need a framework of sensation which includes concepts of tactile stimulation, retinal stimulation, etc. We are not talking here about three chairs, but about one chair—the chair I'm sitting on—and three modes in which it can be investigated.

Even though I am not really arguing for a particular analysis of language here beyond the claim that whatever the analysis it must include our dependence on language and culture, the brief description of language given thus far does suggest three answers to Cultural Relativism, answers which show the possibility of intercultural dialogue as well as the means for keeping objectivity and universality in knowledge.

The first answer to Cultural Relativism is this: language may influence the knowledge we have about the world, but, additionally, it also provides the very tools which enable us to seek knowledge about the world. Without a systematic

11. The most comprehensive investigation into language, intersubjectivity and the creation of alternative conceptual frameworks is provided by Wilfrid Sellars. A good introduction to his work is his early book, *Science, Perception and Reality* (London: Routledge & Kegan Paul, 1963).

way of classifying and codifying our experience, we could not posit or even conceive of underlying uniformities and patterns in the world.

The fact that all human languages are not the same, that concepts and categories differ from group to group, may not have to mean that knowledge must be culturally relative. Such tools as metaphor and analogy,[12] for example, can enable us to reach beyond existing beliefs and enter or create conceptual frameworks unlike our own everyday framework. The work of Benjamin Whorf is a classic example of this. Much of his work seeks to reproduce for us the world of the Native American tribe of the Hopi as well as other, quite different, cultures. He uses linguistic categories as a basis for approximating the world as the Hopi sees it and experiences it.[13] That this is accomplished, that he can make comprehensible a world quite different from our own, reinforces the belief that we are not confined or condemned to the framework of dominant American concepts and conventions.

At this point we need to take a closer look at the insistence on relativism by social scientists such as Whorf and Benedict. They all, at some time in their work, explicitly state that their observations of culture show the folly of seeking universality. But when Benedict offers her conclusions—e.g., "Morality differs in every society and is a convenient term for socially approved habits"[14]—she asserts this claim universally. I doubt that any of the social scientists intend to

---

12. Jonathan Miller's book, *The Body in Question* (New York: Random House, 1979), offers a convincing argument for the role played by analogy in extending our knowledge.

13. A representative sample of Whorf's work can be found in *Language, Thought and Reality: Selected Writings of B.L. Whorf*, ed. J.B. Carroll (Cambridge: MIT Press, 1956). Also, for similar work in this area see Franz Boas, ed., *Handbook of American Indian Languages* (Washington, D.C.: Government Printing Office, 1911–22), and Edward Sapir, *Language: An Introduction to the Study of Speech* (New York: Harcourt Brace Co., 1921).

14. Margaret Mead, ed., *An Anthropologist at Work: Writings of Ruth Benedict* (Boston: Houghton Mifflin Co., 1959), p. 276.

suggest that claims to knowledge can be *both* universal and relative.

It's more likely that they are failing to distinguish cultures and persons as *objects of knowledge* from the *conditions under which knowledge is possible*. This brings us to our second answer to Cultural Relativism: descriptive statements about a culture are not the same as prescriptive statements about which beliefs one should accept or what one should do. Consider the sentence:

A: Material acquisition and consumption is the measure of success.

This statement would be true with respect to the dominant beliefs and practices in the contemporary United States, but would be false with respect to the beliefs and practices of members of an Amish community. If we want A to have a consistent truth value, as suggested in Chapter Three, we should restate the sentence more completely as:

A': Material acquisition and consumption is the measure of success for the majority of people living in the United States in the twentieth century.

The truth conditions remain the same whether A' is asserted by Rockefeller, a member of the Amish community or a Buddhist monk.

A is ambiguous. Does it just mean to *describe* a dominant American practice or does it mean to suggest that material acquisition and consumption *should* constitute a measure of success for all people? A', on the other hand, is clearly a descriptive statement of American culture and is included in our body of empirical knowledge as such. It is objective, for it depicts an actual practice in the world, and it is universal, for it is capable of being correctly asserted by any person.

If we want to talk about whether this is a good or desirable measure of success, we move out of the milieu of anthropology and into the world of philosophy. In other words, social scientists offer valuable methodological tools that can be universally applied as well as valuable insights into the actual workings of different cultures, groups and persons. But it is not within the purview of these disciplines to also formulate criteria by which to judge whether particular cultural practices and beliefs *should* be universally followed and adopted. Taking on this task was just the thing that got early anthropologists and others into trouble (cf. Section 17). And, as we have seen, Benedict and Marx themselves offer the very means of avoiding this difficulty by separating the descriptive work from the prescriptive.[15]

Philosophers themselves, as well, have failed to respond adequately to this distinction. The absence of inquiry into the problem of intersubjectivity [can the conventional "agreements" within a community inform us of a world beyond that community?] has had the effect of inviting Cultural Relativists to fill the gap. In other words, philosophy has traditionally failed to offer clear guidelines which we can use to assess our cultural dependence and begin to transcend it. (For the most part knowledge has been *assumed* to be culturally independent and most analyses forget to offer us the means by which we can begin untangling ourselves from cultural presupposition and prejudice.) Cultural Relativism, on the other hand, does acknowledge this dependence and

---

15. To reiterate briefly, "prescriptive" of course refers to prescribing, in this case telling members of a community what they *should* do, (whether or not they already perform these actions). Hence, part of the prescriptive work of philosophers is arguing for what is right or good, showing why one course of action is preferable to another, evaluating the worth of any code of action. That something is customarily the case does not, ideally, enter the analysis. The primary consideration in formulating prescriptions is to uncover the intrinsic worth of an action. In Section 17 above, we argued for the worth of the methodological prescriptions of Benedict and Marx and showed the value of universally applying their prescriptions. The descriptive work, as we've said, is simply a list of what is already being approved or done in a given culture. An interesting controversy known as the "is/ought" question is found throughout ethical literature: to put it in terms of our discussion, the question is whether the fact that there *is* an existing practice or belief carries any implication of whether there *ought* to be that practice or belief.

though it may overstate the case (and generate unfortunate abuses as we have seen), we at least feel that relativism is talking about *our* world and *our* concerns.

Hence, the third answer to Cultural Relativism is this: it is not enough to say that we *are* culturally dependent; at best this can only promote "investigation" yielding a list of cultural beliefs; at the worst this can further entrench harmful prejudices and practices. But showing the nature and extent of our dependence *does* bring philosophy face to face with the necessity of determining the *role* of culture in empirical knowledge.

If the philosopher takes up this challenge, does that mean then that we must abandon the quest for culturally independent empirical knowledge? Several points made thus far suggest not: Sellers, for example, shows us the possibility of extending ourselves conceptually without denying the role of culture; Whorf and others have been able to reconstruct for us "worlds" that are radically different from our own, worlds which offer us new means of evaluating our own beliefs and practices as well as new data with which to supplement our existing body of empirical knowledge; and, if we can keep confirmation and explanation intact as tools of evidence (without allowing them to be weakened by Cultural Relativism), we should be able to get a clearer picture of where cultural interest promotes investigation or inhibits it.

Here we anticipate a fourth answer to Cultural Relativism: we must give up too much valuable scientific knowledge (in subsuming such knowledge under cultural belief) to justify adopting relativism. Where it may be appropriate and desirable to scrutinize the cultural biases and presuppositions present in scientific investigation, it seems wholly inappropriate and undesirable to dismiss the results of such investigation out of hand.

Beyond the specific conclusions reached by scientists, beyond the range of hypotheses and experimentation, science is able to offer a great deal to us. The world around me, that I live in, appears to me reasonably stable, substantial and predictable. I depend to a large degree on this stability and continuity. As I drive to school, the road remains firmly and reassuringly solid. I expect that it will be so when I drive home this evening. My chair does not collapse under me, the colleague I greet coming down the hall stays embodied the entire distance, my bookshelves continue to hold my books where I put them, my typewriter remains positioned on my desk. In other words, I share with the scientist the presupposition that there is a world independent of my being, a world independent even from the fads and transitory fashions of culture, and a world that can be known.

I seem already to have acquired a fairly reliable and practical body of knowledge about this world: I can manipulate raw material—wood, clay—into enduring objects, I can reglue the rungs of my chair to strengthen it, I can put air into my bicycle tire and ride more comfortably down the road. This world independent of my being is neither alien nor mysterious (though there is a vast amount we don't know or understand in it). The investigation of scientists, the positing of molecules and quarks, does not alter or deprive me of my familiar world of chairs and bicycles, though the investigation may inspire me to understand how molecules generate sufficient strength to constitute dense, resistent physical objects.

The fact that scientific investigation proceeds with such tools as confirmation and explanation is also eminently reassuring. Confirmation provides some basis for my faith in the reliability of my beliefs about the world; that I am able to predict this event or that reassures me that there must be a world independent of myself that *can* be known (regardless of how accurate my actual beliefs are). Successful prediction must at least indicate that my beliefs aren't totally groundless.

Explanation enables me to experiment with competing theories and hypotheses about the world without disrupting the predictability of my own familiar world. For the present, in any case, confirmation and explanation provide some means other than outright prejudice or faith to uphold the beliefs on which we act. They are *capable* also of generating well-founded generalizations about uniformities in and characteristics of the world. I do not have to be helplessly dependent on popular cultural beliefs, but have the means—in confirmation and explanation—of *discriminating the worth* of one belief from the worth of another and *selecting on demonstrable grounds* one belief or hypothesis over another. In this way, whether our beliefs are ultimately right or wrong, we are freed from the indiscriminate acceptance of belief encouraged by relativism.

CHAPTER FIVE
Empirical Knowledge

22. A Modification

My defense of objectivity and universality in knowledge can only go so far. Ultimately, as with any investigation, the data is gathered, the arguments given, and the scope of the inquiry is defined. You are then left to decide: (1) whether the concept of knowledge as true, justified belief, with modification, enables you to distinguish knowledge from opinion, prejudice from fact; and (2) whether you feel the challenge of relativism has been adequately met.

The position that I have taken, thus far, is that the criterion of true, justified belief can provide us with knowledge that is reliable, that does capture the character of our experiences in the world, that does promote investigation and inhibit prejudice. Though we depend heavily on subjective evidence for much of our knowledge, the requirement that our belief must be shown to be objective and universal allows us to move gradually from the subjective realm of feeling and belief to the objective world of chairs and dogs, attitudes and practices.

The criterion proposed by the Naive Relativist in Chapter Two rejected both objectivity and universality and appealed solely to subjective belief. This gives us a fairly easy guideline to use in checking our beliefs, for knowledge becomes whatever we believe or feel at any given moment: I do feel resistance against my leg; Jones does feel that pornography is harmful. (We saw, though, that Naive Relativists are not always so careful with what they claim; these statements sometimes turn into "Here is a chair" and "Pornography *is* harmful"—*without* justification.)

On the one hand, it is not difficult to see why the criterion proposed by the Naive Relativist is inadequate: our body of knowledge becomes highly personal and idiosyncratic (and hence fairly useless for any sort of dialogue or investigation), and the position taken by the Naive Relativist does not really reflect our ordinary expectations of what knowledge should be (namely something true and verifiable). We saw, on the other hand, that the nonrelativist philosopher's use of subjective evidence was very easily confused with the relativist's criterion that knowledge is subjective belief. The Naive Relativist, however, did try to conform to the philosopher's criterion in asserting only true (although subjective) claims as knowledge.

In this way, Naive Relativism showed the need to modify the criterion used by the nonrelativist philosopher. Instead of emphasizing the certainty of subjective statements, the philosopher needs to include the principles by which subjective statements become evidence for statements about the world. Feeling resistance against my leg doesn't in and of itself direct my attention to a chair in my path; but the beliefs we share, such as the belief that:

G: Feelings of resistance indicate the presence of a dense object,

(and that this object here has the appearance of a chair) do enable us to move easily from subjective response to the public world.

We take such general beliefs of the "community" for granted and might wonder why we should bother to make them explicit. One of the problems facing Naive Relativism (and indeed often facing philosophers as well) is this difficulty in accounting for the empirical knowledge we *do* have beyond our own private and personal experiences. In making explicit the general beliefs of a given community or culture, we can (1) account for the manner in which we perceive and shape the world, (2) understand the private sensations and feelings of others which give rise to their statements, and (3) independently investigate and evaluate the worth of the general beliefs of our linguistic community.

Notice that in rejecting the criterion of knowledge offered by the Naive Relativist, we do not reject the importance of an individual's beliefs, opinions, feelings, hopes, aspirations. If anything they are made more important since we now understand their role in bringing us to knowledge of the world.

Once our attention has been turned to this "outer" world, we can begin exploring what this world is like. Our descriptions of this world depict what we see around us, what we experience, the relationships between things, events and our own interactions with the world. The criterion of knowledge as true, justified belief traditionally supports the presupposition that we *can* accurately represent the world in our knowledge claims. We can, in a sense, "read" the external world correctly and report what we read in our statements. This, you might recall, was the position taken by the Context Representationist (the nonrelativist) in Chapter Three. Both our traditional conception of knowledge *and* our ordinary way of looking at things contain the nonrelativistic expectation that objects, events, and situations are "presented" to us. Further, what we are presented with from the world will provide the means by which we can judge the truth of a statement: "If you don't think there's water in the pool, take a look," "Of course the U.S. is in recession; with high unemployment, high interest rates and rising consumer prices, what else would you call it?"

The criterion proposed by the Context Relativist, on the other hand, was that knowledge is immediate acquaintance with a particular, nonreproducible situation. Even a seemingly noncontroversial statement such as "Here is a typewriter," says the relativist, has fluctuating truth values—true at one time, false at another. Today I might say "Here is my typewriter" with a heavy sigh (hence, really saying "Here is my typewriter and I sure don't want to work"), tomorrow I am quite likely to enthusiastically exclaim, "Wow, here is my typewriter" as I eagerly sit down to work (hence, today's statement becomes false tomorow). Maybe I'm not even referring to a particular object: perhaps I'm a secret agent who has been instructed to say "Here is a typewriter" when my mission is complete. We don't, says the relativist, just "neutrally" report what is in the world; whatever we say carries some special significance in a particular situation.

Though we were unable to adopt, in Chapter Three, the Context Relativist's criterion of knowledge, the relativist has considerably deepened our understanding of knowledge and objectivity. First, in identifying the problem of fluctuating truth values, the relativist turned our attention to how truth conditions are determined (by what is in the world). Secondly, by offering compelling examples in which truth values *did* fluctuate, we were able to identify an ambiguity in such statements and thus were able to propose universal truth conditions for the implicit, nonambiguous statements. Thirdly, the careful attention given to the variables of a context by the relativist provided us with the valuable distinction between enduring and informative variables and trivial or idiosyncratic variables; with this distinction we are led, by the relativist, to knowledge of existing practices and patterns in our world. Fourthly, the relativist's stress on the importance of context in the determination of truth conditions reminds us that the knowledge we seek is in no way ethereal and eternal in the sense of being remote from our everyday experience. The knowledge we seek is of the daily world we live in, itself corruptible and changeable, mundane as well as sometimes mysterious.

Thus far, then, we have modified our traditional criterion of knowledge to include the general beliefs of our linguistic community or culture which enable us to use our subjective sensations and beliefs to justify our claims to knowledge. The traditional criterion has been left intact with respect to the expectation that we are, by and large, presented with objects and situations that we can correctly describe and represent in knowledge claims.

But our traditional criterion of knowledge comes under its severest attack with popular Cultural Relativism. The relativist correctly insists that the general beliefs we appeal to in using subjective statements as evidence are themselves culturally reflective, perhaps as representative of cultural prejudice and values as of the world they seek to describe.

The problem illuminated by Cultural Relativism is not just a problem with the traditional criterion of knowledge. The position of Cultural Relativism is deeply responsive to our desire to know the world and people in the world, responsive in a way ignored by nonrelativistic analyses of knowledge. Our recognition of our social and linguistic dependence is acknowledged by the relativist and the position of relativism captures for us an *essential* part of our experience. Though we may resist such dependence or be confused by the extent of such dependence, it is so large a part of how we know the world that any philosophical discussion of knowledge must consider it seriously.

But the nonrelativist philosopher has offered little discussion of this dependence. In this one sense, classical theories of knowledge have been unusually remote from our daily experience. A criterion of knowledge is usually presented to us as if we were unincorporated beings in the world, beings who easily shed their daily concerns and preoccupations in the pursuit of Truth. This is much like asking a person to stop being human, to become, perhaps, a disembodied mind in order to grasp objective reality.

In the face of this lack of response and discussion of our deep-seated dependence on our social world, relativism offers its most formidable challenge to traditional philosophical analyses.[1] I have held, in this book, that relativism—as

---

1. I should mention that the humanistic traditions of existentialism and phenomenology are not so unresponsive. For the most part, the position of existentialism is not represented in our ordinary conception of knowledge (nor is existentialism primarily interested in offering an account of knowledge). Phenomenology, on the other hand, does offer an alternative

valuable as it is in pointing out weaknesses in our conception of knowledge and offering an apparent remedy—is too extreme to adopt. It fails to provide a framework of investigation. It generates serious abuses. It undermines the very independence of thought we seek.

On the other hand, the failure of popular relativism to truly account for our knowledge of the world does not diminish its value and its critical role in modifying our conception of knowledge. The two modifications which relativism correctly insists upon are, as we have seen: (1) the need to include in our analysis of knowledge explicit means of using subjective statements as evidence for objective claims about the world. To include something like the principles of evidence discussed in Chapter Two would satisfy this need. (Principles of evidence, you might recall, may be the general beliefs used by the linguistic community, beliefs such as "Such-and-so physical stimulation indicates the presence of such-and-so object.")

(2) In recognizing that the concepts and general beliefs we use in coming to know the world reflect considerable cultural influence, our analysis of knowledge must both acknowledge this influence and insist upon close examination of these concepts and beliefs. No account of knowledge should assume that the conceptual framework (the concepts we use to describe the world) is free from bias and ill-founded generalizations. Also, given the status and prestige of political power and material wealth in our own culture, we may want to see which of our shared beliefs exist only to further the power and control of those protecting or promoting only their own interest: "What's good for GM is good for America."

---

account of knowledge and, under some interpretations, is thought to provide justification for Cultural Relativism. The part of phenomenology that has entered our daily thought is the account of the fluid, elastic character of our perception—the fact that we bring to perception our hopes, expectations, etc., which become part of the horizon through which we perceive the world beyond us. This fits naturally and easily into our normal encounters with the world and how we see it.

Putting the very conceptual framework of our culture into question, so to speak, emphasizes our own role as "knowers." To be a knower is to perceive the world around us, to make judgments about what is in the world, to evaluate the merits of one belief over another, to assert our critical opinion of practices and attitudes in the world. As knowers we are not simply passive recipients of cultural beliefs and values. As knowers we are active, engaged persons in the world, subject to enormous influence from culture and community, who exercise in our own right considerable influence on others and on the shape of the world.

We ask of our criterion of knowledge that it help to dispel confusion about our role as knowers, that it enables us to distinguish the valuable and justified beliefs we hold from the worthless and unjustified beliefs, that it permit knowledge of the world rather than flagrant skepticism. In order for our criterion to meet these needs, it does seem that our conception of knowledge must be modified in the ways suggested here.

23. Dialogue with the Popular Relativist

In this section I will review the important terrain of one's personal judgments and identity, for relativism is often mistaken as the only position which promotes individuality and supports the legitimacy of personal opinion, thus allowing us to say things like: "For me, jogging is the road to good health," "I just can't quit smoking cold turkey," "I would rather decide for myself about whom to vote for." Thus far, our emphasis has been on using personal beliefs and preferences to lead us to the objective world and evaluation of that world. However, each one of us is an object in the world, an object whose actions and beliefs can be described, and perhaps included in knowledge claims.[2]

---

2. There is controversy about whether any statement using "indexicals"—references to this particular time or place or speaker—can be a legitimate item of empirical knowledge; hence my qualification. We can, however, understand descriptions of persons on a par with descriptions of objects.

Personal description is the very heart of much of our investigation in the social sciences. Though it is illegitimate for us to generalize from just our own experiences, sociologists and psychologists are able to amass many personal descriptions and from them generalize and formulate existing trends, attitudes and preferences which do help us to increase our understanding of the world around us. If I cultivate the skill of identifying *my own responses* accurately, I am able to offer substantive data to researchers and, more importantly, I am better able to anticipate my own desires and inclinations so that I might be able to be more satisfied with what I do. Such skill—the ability to recognize my own responses—is not to be taken lightly. Two current modes of expression reveal our ineptness in this domain. The first is the tendency to generalize when we should be offering a description of our own preferences. For example, we might have heard ourselves say: "Driving cross-country is (always) exhilarating" or "Mathematical formulae are (necessarily) difficult to understand." Neither statement is true, whereas "I find driving cross-country exhilarating" and "I have trouble understanding mathematical formulae" might well be true.

There is a second mode of reporting often confused with self-expression. With the advent and popularity of encounter group therapy, we have been led to think we are being "honest" when we verbally attack another person: "You are an insensitive boor," "I've always thought you were irritating." Psychologists tend not to encourage this misconception of honesty. They are more likely to lead the speaker to report his/her own feelings (rather than to validate the indictment of another person): "I felt hurt when you forgot my birthday," "I find myself wanting to get up and leave when you begin talking about your old boyfriends; I feel as though I'm being asked to compete with them." Compare these two versions of "honesty": the latter offers accurate information about the speaker; the former, in a sense, dismisses the target with a harsh judgment, offering no information whatsoever. The benefits of coming to identify your own responses should be obvious: communication with others is greatly enhanced and you have the chance to reflect upon your reaction to this person or situation, to recognize familiar patterns in your responses, to assess whether these patterns enable you to live the life you want.

Hence not only are personal experiences, feelings and beliefs important in coming to know the world (as discussed in Chapter Two), but descriptions of such experiences are valuable in their own right, both in acquainting ourselves with others and in coming to know our own expectations and intricacies. The mode in which personal experience is conveyed in literature, diaries and poetry shows how valuable a resource it is. Thus, my rejection of Naive Relativism as a philosophical position does not include a rejection of the value of personal experience descriptions.

"Okay," you might say, "I understand how persons can be objects of knowledge, but how on earth are the descriptions of such persons universal?" "Much in the same way," a nonrelativist might answer, "that descriptions of objects are universal: anyone observing you in this situation will be able to say 'Smith certainly doesn't like spinach.' " Though another observer might not be able to give a comprehensive description of you, your likes and dislikes, opinions and moods, will manifest themselves in your behavior. Depending on how transparent you are or how guarded, another person will be able to discover your shyness or your passion for Chinese food or your fear of heights. Much about you is available for "public," objective description, which can be a source of valuable information. Allowing others to know you can provide something of a safeguard against self-deception, for very often friends can see (and point out to you) patterns in your behavior that you might not want to continue. Having "observers" around us can certainly promote self-knowledge and offers a reflection of ourselves otherwise unavailable. The point here, however, is simply to note that for a statement to be universal doesn't always mean that it will depict some generality in the world; it may also mean that any observer will be able to make true statements about you or about this situation.

But of course we don't want to talk only about individual things or individual persons. We are also interested in the

issues and vital concerns, patterns and uniformities in the
world as well as in enlarging our own perception and appreciation of the world. When Smith says "I just don't like
country music," Jones might well respond with, "Okay, but
listen to this particular piece. I think it has a nice beat which
sounds like the blues you listen to; I also like these lyrics
for they seem to say what I feel when I want to talk to you
and you're not home." So Smith listens and is able to
distinguish this beat and these lyrics. Whether or not Smith
comes to enjoy country music, the music is objectively present
in the world and Jones offers the means by which a listener
(any listener) *might* come to appreciate it. Without this arena
of objectivity and Jones's (desire for) universality, Smith might
remain unnecessarily limited in the pleasure she can derive
from the world.

Though we have ultimately rejected Naive Relativism,
viewing it as incapable of offering a complete account of
knowledge, there is a realm of "personal knowledge" that
should be respected. This, of course, is the realm of your
decisions, actions, goals, dreams, hopes, what you feel good
about, how you present yourself. It is very often easy to
confuse the opinion of "authorities"—teachers, parents, a
boss—with your own preferences. The heated debates in the
sixties and seventies about how long a man should wear his
hair and whether beards, mustaches and sideburns were
acceptable, helped us to become aware of and to define this
area of personal control.

Obviously, as our actions extend beyond ourselves, we do
accept limits, moderate constraints, on what we want to do.
You may wait, for example, to buy a new shirt until your
bills are paid. Some constraints, of course, are not always
legitimate. My friends think pinball is childish; but the pleasure I derive from playing pinball is real and need not be
restrained (unless I am spending more time at the arcade
than at the typewriter). My likes and dislikes can and should
be respected even though they may not have universal appeal
or approval. To accept that knowledge claims should be
universal and objective does not diminish our own realm of
decision and control. The subjective world of Smith and

Jones, of you and I, is real and should be known and explored. The more you insist on the right to exercise control of your subjective world, the more likely you will be to respect the rights of others to exercise the same control over their subjective "worlds."

But, you might well ask, all along in this discussion you've been insisting that justified belief is preferable to unjustified belief, suggesting that the former has some sort of authority and *should* be accepted over unjustified belief. Does this mean that the authority had by knowledge claims (in being true) has the right to tell me what to believe or what to do?

In one sense, yes it does. If you and a friend are going by train into the city to see a show, the last train you can take and still make the first act is the 4:02. Your friend says "I don't think the train will come at 4:02 today—I bet it will come at 5:02, so we don't have to hurry." You pull out a schedule and point to 4:02, you call the station and let your friend listen to the report that the train is running on time. At this point you feel that your friend is *obliged* to accept the claim that the last afternoon train to the city leaves at 4:02 and you should hasten to meet the train (if you are to get to the theater on time).

We might say that the authority had by knowledge claims is the authority of being right, of being verifiable by any knower, of providing a reasonable basis for action.[3] It's not often that this authority conflicts with the authority exercised by you, as we talked about above, in making your own decisions; usually the two areas work in tandem: you will appeal and depend on your knowledge of the world to plan the best course of action to achieve some goal.

But what if the two areas do conflict? Let's consider the classic dilemma of the smoker. One *knows* the lethal effects

---

3. The train example is misleading in the sense of suggesting that knowledge claims have some sort of "absolute" authority. To dispel any confusion here, the authority had by knowledge claims only *obliges* us, it does not *compel* us, to accept what is asserted. What this obligation may entail is spelled out in more detail in the example beginning in the next paragraph in the text.

of tar and nicotine on the human system, one *knows* the
polluting effect of smoke on the environmnent as well as
on the health of others, one *knows* that smoking makes one
neither glamorous nor sophisticated nor independent. At the
same time, one *desires* the effects (whether soothing or en-
ergizing) of smoking, one *enjoys* the taste and sensations
involved in inhaling, one *wants* to continue the pleasures
accompanying smoking. It seems, of course, that this is a
personal decision: if I want to ruin my body, I have the
right to do so.

As many have pointed out, it's not so personal when
others suffer ill effects from your choice. Still, there is no
argument that the difficult process of quitting is *wholly* on
your shoulders. No one else, no matter how concerned, is
able to change your desires, wants and enjoyments; no one
else is able to choose for you not to light up in a given
instance; no one else can live through the withdrawal symptoms (though they may have to live with them). To return
now to the original dilemma, knowledge is supposed to have
the authority of justification and offer guidance to right action.
We are, as we saw above, obliged to accept justified belief
(e.g., "To enjoy good health, one shouldn't smoke") over
unjustified belief (e.g., "Smoking doesn't harm anyone").
However, in this case the obligation doesn't seem to be
compelling enough to cause you to relinquish the pleasures
of smoking. (I suspect that many cases of prejudice might
be similar.)

There are two "answers," neither surprising, which can
help us assess the extent to which objective knowledge
becomes a compelling subjective concern: (1) The knowledge
we have about the effects of smoking does serve to put one's
smoking (and desires) into question, into "public" question,
as it were. In this sense the authority of the knowledge that
smoking is damaging to the environment and the health of
others does oblige the smoker to minimize public pollution
and the imposition on others as much as possible. We might,
somewhat idealistically, expect the smoker to also feel obliged
to take on the task of disentangling him/herself from the
addiction.

But this "personal" obligation is not usually accepted, at least not to the extent of truly making the smoker want to quit. It seems, from the accounts of many smokers, that only when they *feel* the detrimental effects of smoking will they begin to be affected by, to consider seriously, the objective data available. (How quickly a smoker will respond to feeling the effects will vary; some will take action immediately upon noticing a shortness of breath when they run, others might wait until they are quite ill.)

A similar conflict appears in our ongoing debate on pornography. We can imagine Smith saying to Jones (Jones being the critic of pornography): "What gives you the right to judge this situation [of a woman being pictured in bondage, for example, and enjoying it] when the woman chooses to put herself in that situation, may be genuinely enjoying it, and you have the choice not to view it?" What gives Jones and me (and Smith as well) the right to judge is the fact that though I may not view these kinds of pictures nor do I myself derive pleasure from them, I live in a world where others do view these pictures, do derive pleasure from them and are encouraged by them to view women as appropriate objects of domination—an attitude that will affect my relations with others and the respect I expect to receive from (as well as offer to) others.

These examples seem to suggest, then, the general conclusion that there is a legitimate area in which objective knowledge can constrain one's actions (at least when this objective knowledge is enforced by the community). For the most part, these are constraints which we normally accept and feel are reasonable.

However, the second "answer" to the question of when objective knowledge can change our subjective choices acknowledges the fact that objective (and universal) knowledge does not seem to be able to prompt, in and of itself, relevant action, particularly in the case of the smoker. Only when objective knowledge (or an objective situation) alters one's subjective "world," does such knowledge become compelling: when one feels short of breath, when Smith hears a male friend proclaim, "She just needs a good whack to keep her in line." This may account, in part, for the relativist's insistence on subjective knowledge. What the Naive Relativist does not distinguish is the fact that the objective knowledge which affects our subjective choices is not the same as the subjective opinions and feelings we started out with in Chapter Two: the beliefs and feelings about the world we are talking about here have been scrutinized, examined, challenged, modified, discarded or accepted in the public arena. They "return" to us justified, complete and nonambiguous, freer from prejudice than many of our original beliefs, and with a kind of guarantee—so far as we are able to determine—that they are *worthy* of acceptance. Without the insistence on objectivity and universality in knowledge, we would have no means of distinguishing the worth of one belief from that of another. In other words, left with the subjective knowledge of the Naive Relativist we have, then, only a fairly mixed bag of beliefs, perhaps prejudiced, perhaps contradictory, some perhaps right (but which ones?) on which to base our actions.

As we saw in Chapter Three, moving into the realm of the objective world does not always guarantee freedom from the limitations of popular relativism in our thought. We saw that the relativist conceived of "context" in terms of the uniqueness of a given situation, the immediately apparent variables of the present: the mood of a situation, the intent of the speaker, the chance remark. On the other hand, Sosa, Hegel and Aristotle (as well as Benedict and Marx in Chapter Four) argued for a much broader conception of context: the present was seen as arising from the objective concerns of an investigation, from an existing situation in the world, from recognizable social or historical or economic conditions, from dominant cultural practices. In other words, whatever is going on *right now* gains its *primary* meaning or significance from ongoing practices in the world, existing conditions, entrenched cultural belief and interpretation. (The relativist, you might recall, wants to insist that the significance of the present originates with some unique variable of the present.)

The controversy between the "narrow" interpretation of context and the "broader" conception used by the nonrelativist was vividly illustrated in the brief exchange between Mike Wallace and Frank Terpil described at the end of Chapter Three. Terpil offered, in effect, the popular appeal to "The end justifies the means" to justify his actions. This is an instance of the popular relativist's narrow interpretation of context: the context in this cliché is "the end" of a single endeavor, the outcome of an action, the realization of a particular goal. In Terpil's case, "making a buck" was offered as the end—*the sole criterion*—by which he felt his actions (of selling arms to unstable countries) should be justified. (Terpil's reasoning, we should note, is the same as that often used in our daily thought and action.)

Wallace rejected this narrow conception of context and, in his questioning, introduced the broader conception of context used by the nonrelativist of Chapter Three, namely, that Terpil's actions (the "means" by which he made his buck) had consequences beyond the "end" and that his actions should be judged according to the criteria of moral worth and the effect of his actions on the larger community. In effect, Wallace moved the focus of the inquiry to include "that to which a thing is relative," rejecting Terpil's claim that his actions are relative to this particular end and insisting instead that his actions must be evaluated relative to their public (objective) consequences. Just as, in Chapter Three, we were unable to universalize the student's appeal to the "special needs" of his situation, so we are unable to universalize Terpil's appeal to making a buck.

Having objective consequences, as we saw in the earlier examples, gives Wallace (and other nonrelativists) the right to reject the appeal to special consideration. In other words, if I will be affected, I have the right to judge and modify your actions. Additionally, as we saw, we are brought to a recognition of compelling problems in the world when we appeal to the broader conception of context. We are able to see the more substantial variables which constitute this situation or that. Just as the student's appeal forced us to consider our attitudes and practices about education, so does Terpil's appeal make us question our own casual acceptance of "making a buck" as the sole justification of action. His appeal should also turn our attention to the increasing frequency of handling political as well as personal crises by violent means.

Following the recommendation of the nonrelativists (among whom I include both Benedict and Marx, though neither might approve), being able to see the particular features of the present situation ("a relative thing") as significant within a larger context of social attitudes or economic practices ("that to which a thing is relative") gives us a sound and substantial means by which to understand our daily, changing world. It also enables us to deal with the Gestalt character of our experience.[4] As we saw, we don't experience situations in fragments (whether in sensory fragments of touch, sound, smell, taste or sight or in a single feature of the situation being more vivid than the rest). No single variable (however unique) seems to present itself as the sole determination of meaning or truth. Rather, our experience is of an integrated whole, within which particular features are seen as belonging to a pattern or continuity in the world and in our lives. The analysis of the popular relativist "deprives" us of a way to account for this integrated character of our experience and our deep involvement with the objective world. Without an account of our normal mode of perceiving the world, we will be unable to move between the "now" and the continuity giving rise to the "now," we are prevented from recognizing the essential role of human interpretation in the perception and creation of our situation in the world.

In isolating single or unique features of a given situation, the relativist is in danger of inadvertently encouraging fixation

---

4. "Gestalt" refers to the integrated structures or patterns that constitute our experience, the individual features of which cannot be explained apart from the "whole" experience. The use of "Gestalt" here is more general. When, in Chapter Three, we discussed variables of the context—those which were significant, those which were not, those which could generate universal truth conditions and those which could not—we did select specific features and discuss their contribution to the context (thereby suggesting that some independent explanation or analysis is possible). Even with this deviation, I use "Gestalt" to convey the essentially integrated character of our experience.

on a trivial or nonexistent variable. Senator Joseph McCarthy is generally thought to have manipulated minor discomfort with the Cold War (with the USSR in the fifties) into outright fear to make a name for himself and further his political career. We can minimize the recurrence of such manipulation if we are accustomed to seeing the real "question under consideration" in a given situation, if we have a habit of discriminating the vital and relevant variables of a situation from the trivial and idiosyncratic. Popular relativism offers us no such means of discrimination.

The remaining questions a popular relativist might want discussed all involve the individual's relationship to the community, whether to a small group (like the Black Panthers) or to the larger culture in which s/he was raised. We saw in Chapter Four the extent of our dependence on our culture and, to a lesser extent, on the community around us. Such dependence is perceived by some as a threat to one's "individuality," one's independence and identity. Given the importance of our relationship to our culture and community, we will briefly address here some of the confusions or misconceptions about our dependency.

On the one hand, we are dependent on society for education, employment and the means of support, health care and research, protection and assistance. Though we support these services, none of us would be able to offer ourselves or our family this range of institutional opportunity outside a social setting. Chapter Four focuses on our conceptual dependence on society, particularly the means with which we organize our world and lives, means such as our concepts of language, customs and social practices. Again, were we to live outside society, our range of concepts would be severely limited. Most likely our exploration and investigation of the world would be restricted to the concerns of subsistence, and our behavior would be similarly restricted to the primary needs of biological maintenance (leaving little time, as well as imagination, for other modes of human expression such as art and music).

The dependence that we are most keenly aware of, however, is the manner in which our daily lives are interwoven with the activities, expectations and desires of others. We may enjoy this dependency—going to the beach with a friend, having long conversations by the fire, being greeted with a smile and a warm welcome, feeling good about having been able to lend a hand to someone. We may, as well, resent this dependency—feeling obliged to be somewhere at an appointed time, having to account for our whereabouts, feeling our actions are being watched and judged, feeling constrained in the extent to which we can "be ourselves."

Whether we enjoy or resent the social interaction we have, it provides an important medium for our growth and development. We acquire a sense of self, both in the response we get from others and in the variety of human activity surrounding us (which excites our imagination and leads us to assessing which of these activities we would like to pursue). We are continually challenged beyond our present capabilities by the achievements of others (their accomplishments become our possibilities). We are able to develop a substantial and realistic sense of human power as we see the effect we have on others and the effects we can have on the physical world. Exclusive of society, these important and fundamental aspects of ourselves (that we take for granted) would be stunted, if developed at all. From this perspective, the extent to which we can "be ourselves" seems promoted rather than restricted by those around us.

We have little opportunity to realize the extent to which we utilize our social environment to achieve the independence we prize so highly. Media images tend to link independence with aloofness from society. Consider, for example, the image projected by movie stars Charles Bronson or John Wayne—aloof, "self-sufficient" (think about this for a moment), unaffected by the conventions and judgments of the community. Dependence is largely depicted as weakness rather than as an essential part of our human life. Disdain for community activities and goals is the response we are encouraged to associate with independence, rather than appreciation or involvement. The song "I Did It My Way" sentimentalizes this popular conception of "independence," again suggesting that individuality is achieved in opposition to one's social milieu.

This may take some reflection on our part, for we are so accustomed to the mythology surrounding "individuality" and "independence" that to challenge such sentiments seems very radical. Underneath the mythology, however, lies a very real need for a clear definition of self and the opportunity for self-determination, self-expression and self-assertion. Very often, not surprisingly, the only criterion one requires is just to be "different" from all the others. Considering our earlier review of society's contribution to the continued development of our identity, there is some question about what "different" would be.

How, then, does one ever distinguish clearly one's self from the wealth of social and cultural influences? Or is a person simply a complex composite of culturally determined responses? One conception of a person, espoused by some popular Cultural Relativists, is just this, that a person is only and entirely a manifestation of his/her culture. In Chapter Four, however, we saw persons who were able to transcend specific cultural biases, who were able to "step back" from their beliefs and attitudes to critically evaluate these beliefs, who were able to acquaint themselves with radically different cultural beliefs and practices (you might recall Whorf's successful introduction to Hopi and Mayan cultures). It seems, then, that however dependent we are on our culture and community, we are not helpless nor do we seem to be very enfeebled by this dependence.

The original suggestion was that we are, to an important extent, comprised of culturally given attitudes and values, preferences and desires, roles and models which we strive to fulfill. The very appeal of popular Cultural Relativism is its recognition of the extent to which our identity is fashioned by cultural ideals. Such influence might be objectionable if we were merely passive, mechanical reactors to cultural stimuli. What is truly interesting, though, is that we seem to achieve some degree of intellectual and emotional independence by means of the cultural and social conditions around us. The more we utilize the diverse resources of our culture, the more we seem capable of transcending the limitations of that culture.

The *fact* of our dependency on our culture should not mean that we are obliged to adopt every belief, adhere to every custom, condone every practice of our culture. The *fact* of our dependency may mean, though, that we are obliged to scrutinize every belief, judge the extent to which custom promotes or inhibits our well-being, and evaluate the existing practices of our culture. Only in this way does it seem likely that the negative effects of inherent biases and actual restraints in the body of cultural belief will be neutralized.

I realize that the discussion here has pursued what "individuality" and independence are *not*. Though popular Cultural Relativism could not account for a large part of our knowledge, it does offer us the provocative view that individuality and independence cannot be seen as a rejection of one's cultural or social dependence, for the dependence remains as a necessary and integral part of our human identity (though, of course, we may want to reject particular beliefs or practices). Using this valuable claim as a starting point, we may want to consider how individuals can "come into their own" and take on the task of directing their lives and implementing their choices *beyond* the determinations of their culture (rather than in opposition to such influence). As valuable as Cultural Relativism has been in turning our attention towards the fundamental role culture plays in the constitution of our identity, it has not been able to account for our emergence as reflective, critical beings rather than as mechanical reactors to cultural conditioning.

24. A Final Defense of Objectivity and Universality

I said in Chapter One, Section 2, that I would prefer that knowledge be objective and universal. This preference led me to investigate how reasonable this desire was given the challenge of relativism. At that time, I simply made a tentative commitment to such an investigation; I had offered no grounds for my preference and so could not assert that knowledge should be objective and universal.

Much of my argument in favor of pursuing objectivity and universality is contained, of course, in the various responses given to the relativistic positions (e.g., that what one feels can't itself tell us about the world, that truly unique features of a situation are unable to tell us about ongoing practices and changing attitudes in the world, that cultural belief cannot constitute foundations of knowledge). This, however, is incomplete, for we are still left with aspects of our experience that seem to suggest that my pursuit is futile.

Let's consider objectivity first. The classic example against the pursuit of objectivity is that of a car accident with five witnesses. We all know that we'll get five different (often conflicting) descriptions of the accident. Yet, in insisting on objectivity, I am claiming that there is a situation that is recognizable apart from the witnesses' perception of it. We may only be able to know the "objective" situation through the witnesses' reports. But how is this possible if the reports are conflicting?

Similarly, you may question my claim (in Chapter Three) that an artist like Van Gogh depicts the objective world. No, you may say, Van Gogh *adds* something to the world that is not already there. His perception (or conception) of rigid objects as pulsating or, in some sense, animated, does not emanate from the object but from his imagination. How, then, can we possibly claim that Van Gogh's painting is an (accurate) description of something in the world, i.e., that it describes or represents actual characteristics of an object or situation in the world?

Both examples illustrate the necessity of acknowledging the dual character of perception and of our concept of objectivity. Perception, of course, consists partly of the physical stimulation of our sensory organs (the pressure you feel in your seat reminds you that a dense object is supporting you). It also consists of the judgments we make about this sensory information (feeling pressure of this sort must mean that I am seated). Of course we are so accustomed to these physical sensations and what we take them to mean that we never actually stop and think these things consciously. Chapter Two, however, argued that we might want to be aware of the judgments we make in perception, for the general beliefs or principles we appeal to might be fallacious (and thereby will prevent us from accurately describing the world in our knowledge claims).

Similarly, we are reminded in the above examples that our concept of objectivity should include both the (physical) constitution of an object or event *and* the modes in which it can be classified, experienced, interpreted or "seen as" valuable or worthless. Acknowledging that such modes are available to human interpretation should convince us to give up our popular insistence on a "Dragnet" conception of objectivity ("I'm a reporter; I do not judge what I see, I simply report what I see"). To include the role of interpretation in our account of objectivity is a difficult move philosophically. Since we want to know the empirical world that exists apart from human concerns, we seem to undermine our own project by including interpretation. However, we also see that the world is neither experienced nor known apart from human perception and interpretation. The best we seem capable of is to include interpretation in our analysis and to continue to insist on universality in knowledge claims (thereby minimizing the occurrence of unchecked bias).

In the case of the car accident, though, we see that we must be careful about what interpretation we accept. The suggestion in Chapter Three was to include in our account of objectivity only those variables (of which interpretation is included) of a situation which could be *duplicated* by another observer. In the case of the five witnesses, we tend to accept the details of the accident which are the same in all five reports; we assume that all five witnesses could not coincidentally fabricate identical details. Taking into account their various positions, what their attention was on at the time of the accident, how reliable they generally are, we try to determine which features of their reports belong to (or originate from) the actual situation in the world and which belong to their imagination.

On the other hand, we see in the Van Gogh example that the characteristics of objects and events include far more than physical features such as color, shape, size, density. (As we saw in other examples, objects and events are also characterized by their distinctive relations to their surroundings, historical antecedents, cultural values.) Van Gogh's paintings may give an objective representation of how we feel about the world or how we feel in the world: it may feel sinister to us sometimes and we quickly recognize or recall that feeling upon viewing one of his later paintings. The later paintings may offer, beyond what we feel, a view of the natural world *as* powerful, independent and "alive," or a view of nature *as* formidable, fearsome and opaque (compare this with earlier impressionists who characterized nature *as* light, transparent and comfortingly pretty).

Several points here affect our treatment and understanding of objectivity. The first is that we perceive (and conceive) of things or situations *as* this or that: we transform a collection of physical characteristics into the Gestalt character of our experience. We see this resistant, dense, four-legged object *as* a chair and *as a chair* it offers a means of sitting, of obstruction ("Ouch, who left that blasted chair in the doorway!"), of belonging to an aesthetic environment ("Two chairs around that table would look nice"). Just as in the case of the accident, the witnesses received varying degrees of information through their sensory apparatus, their experience was of seeing a collision *as* an accident, feeling shock and numbness upon witnessing serious injury (perhaps seeing human life *as* fragile and transient)—all distinctly human categories essential to our interaction with the world.

A note of caution brings us to the second of our points. The caution is this: even though the objects of our *experience* are transformed by us from mere stimuli to whole objects, events or situations capable of integration and interaction with other objects of our experience, this does not mean that we singlehandedly (or even culturally) create our perceptual world or that we are always "right" in our designation of something *as* this or that. The whole tone of this book reflects this need for caution: human inventiveness and imagination can be as destructive and fallible as they can be necessary and invaluable in coming to know the world. Human belief and judgment, investigation and supposition must *always* be subject to scrutiny and challenge. We have seen how easily we can fall into abusing this human capacity when there is no critical reflection accompanying judgment.

Our second point about objectivity, then, is this. The characteristics we ascribe to objects include both the physical properties that affect us in distinct ways and the modes in which such an object can be experienced or perceived. Hence, our investigation of the world (objects and events in the world) will pursue knowledge of the physical characteristics of an object *along with* our judgments about them. These judgments must be fully explicated in the investigation, in order to be made available to independent scrutiny and examination. Even the most scientific investigations do not elicit "facts" as conceived by reporters, but give to physical data the Gestalt character of experience. That is, an investigator will fit the data into the existing, dominant or popular (familiar) mode of understanding or interpreting the data. Rather than reject such transformations of data, scientists and philosophers would do better to include the relevant presuppositions and interpretations into the results of their investigation.[5]

The third point about objectivity is whether we want to include outright imaginative products which affect our perception of the world, e.g., Van Gogh's later paintings, per-

---

5. I should note that this is a fairly unconventional suggestion, certainly not representative of the dominant views of philosophers. Should this question (of the extent to which human interpretation should be included in our concept of objectivity) interest you, you might want to see how others handle it: e.g., R.M. Chisholm, *Perceiving: A Philosophical Study* (Ithaca: Cornell, 1957); H.H. Price, *Perception* (London: Allen & Unwin, 1932); C.I. Lewis, *Mind and the World Order* (New York: Dover, 1929) (for work in the analytic tradition); E. Husserl, *Experience and Judgment* (Halle, 1922) and E. Casey, *Imagination* (Evanston: Northwestern, 1975) (for work in the phenomenological tradition); and C.S. Peirce, "How to Make Our Ideas Clear" (1940) in *Philosophical Writings of Peirce*, ed. J. Buchler (New York: Dover, 1955) (for work in the pragmatic tradition).

haps, or the categories of "provocative" or "obscene" by which we judge pornography. On the one hand, Van Gogh's imagination has nothing to do with actual characteristics of actual objects in the world. And our quest for objectivity in knowledge has been, all along, to represent what is truly in the world. On the other hand, the way in which pictures are seen as pornographic, provocative or obscene does seem to constitute an actual situation in our world.

To the extent that these characteristics are presented as part of an object or situation in the world (e.g., rhythm emanating from a rigid object, a woman seen as deriving pleasure from humiliation), they have been included in the objective realm. We can assert statements which can be shown to be true or false, universal and objective (or not), verifiable, debatable or unjustified. *So long as a characteristic is asserted as belonging objectively to an object or situation*, it comes under the same (severe) scrutiny as *any other* claim to knowledge. Jones's controversial claim, for example—that deriving pleasure from seeing women in humiliating or compromising situations condones the more pervasive social attitude that women are appropriate objects of humiliation and compromise—may or may not be true. Jones's assertion, however, is that such attitudes *are* present in the world and that certain pornographic pictures *do* condone existing attitudes. We don't merely accept Jones's assertion because it has been given objective form; we look around for confirming or refuting evidence. The point is that our attention is directed to practices in the world and characteristics of our world: this is always the realm of objectivity.

Hence, Van Gogh's "claim" that objects are more than rigid, dense and static things is equally asserted in the objective realm. If he is right, perhaps he deepens our perception and understanding of the world much in the way that molecular theory does. Even though we don't directly perceive the bonding of molecules to form the rigid objects we sit on, we might appreciate knowing how this rigidity comes about and we might marvel at how the bonding of seemingly fragile units like molecules can produce such strength and resistence. Even though we don't directly perceive rhythmic pulsations from rigid objects, we might begin thinking of the effect these objects have on us and how this effect is produced by their impinging on our sensory organs. We might thus be led to a more metaphorical appreciation of the power and intensity of the world around us.

This is, of course, a highly complex relationship with which to deal. Including the products of human imagination and judgment in our concept of objectivity seems to come dangerously close to diluting "objectivity" to the point of worthlessness (i.e., to the point of being indistinguishable from "subjectivity"). However, as complex and as difficult as this relationship is, we can retain the strength of our concept of objectivity so long as we keep clearly in mind that objectivity is representation of the empirical world, that objective statements depict what is in the world. Coming to know this world will surely involve considerable debate and hypothesis, tentative consideration (such as Jones's claim) and modification of what we think we know. But the criterion of objective as what is in fact in the world remains effective as a means of guiding debate and investigation.

The task of philosophers is to define clearly the subjective component in perception and knowledge, so that we are able to make a clearer distinction in our own beliefs as well as acknowledge our own responsibility for situations in the world. We don't want the mythical extreme preoccupying journalists ("I only report what I see"), for that misleads us (and them) into thinking of ourselves as merely passive recipients of raw data. Nor do we want the other extreme (often taken by the popular relativist) that the world is nothing more than human invention, desire, opinion. Rather, to display the human-given properties of objects along with their own physical properties in our analysis enables us to *truly* represent our experience of the world and capture the whole range of attributes which objects and events can take on.

Similarly, the concept of universality in knowledge might seem to you inadequately defended, particularly since much of our discussion emphasized *agreement* among observers, both in the concepts used and the judgments made in a given situation. It would seem that the considerable *disagreement* around us would be enough, then, to show the impossibility of achieving universality in knowledge claims. Jones's claim about how women are sometimes depicted in pornography is asserted universally as well as objectively: he is saying not only does this practice exist in the world and affect our attitudes, but *anyone* taking a close look will come to see this. Since there is considerable disagreement about Jones's claim, doesn't this mean that his statement is not universal and therefore can't ever be shown to be true or false?

This gives us the opportunity to clear up a possible misunderstanding (that I myself have encouraged, perhaps). Universality does not fundamentally rest on simple agreement in a community, though in Chapter Four we saw that intersubjective agreement would enable us to eventually show universality. Rather, agreement itself rests on the fact that one position can be shown to be preferable to another, one claim stronger than another, one belief more worthy than another. As we mentioned earlier in this chapter, knowledge claims have a kind of authority that comes with being right, being verifiable and capable of offering us a reliable basis for action. Whether or not we like or approve or resent or want to ignore this authority, we are—as knowers in the world—obliged (but not compelled) to accept this authority. If Jones, for example, is able to show fairly conclusively that pornography does diminish our concept of women as persons, we are obliged (however reluctantly) to seek to develop erotic literature and pleasure which does not depend upon another's helplessness or humiliation. As we debate with Jones on whether or not these practices and attitudes exist objectively in the world, we may also be considering what we *want* in the world. Smith, for example, wants to promote erotic pleasure and the possibility of such pleasure for everyone in the world. She is seeking, then, to offer a universal principle, just as Jones seeks to universally insure dignity and respect for all persons in the world. These principles of actions should not conflict nor contradict one another (for then they would not be truly universal): Smith may have to consider forms of erotica which promote seeing others with dignity and give up forms which exploit or diminish the way we see others.

Hence universality in our knowledge claims does not, at bottom, depend on agreement among knowers, but on strength of justification. Again, even though subjective opinions and concerns may be instrumental in gathering the evidence, arguing for or against a position, the test of universality, is not the strength of one's personal feelings but the strength of the belief itself.

At this point our investigation of relativism and knowledge comes to a natural end. However, as with the other chapters, I can't leave you with the feeling that all our questions are answered, all our problems solved. A large question about the whole enterprise needs to be introduced and I will leave you with this question to consider. "Why," some readers have asked, "can't knowledge be both objective and relative? Why can't some knowledge claims be objective and universal and others relative? Why must you insist that the same criterion of knowledge apply to so many diverse kinds of knowledge claims?"

My belief is that without a universal criterion of knowledge, we have no assurance—or possibility of assurance—that *any* of our beliefs are truly knowledge. For example, "Water freezes at 32° Fahrenheit" and "God loves you" might appear to be as extreme and diverse as one can get in the range of things we claim to know in our world. The relativist might well think it unfair to dismiss "God loves you" on the grounds that thus far proof of God's existence and attributes rests largely on faith rather than demonstration. This, the relativist might say, just goes to show how much you'll miss out on if you insist that *all* knowledge claims have to be *shown* to be objective and universal.

And I would reply, I have no intention of asking you to discard a belief that clearly enhances your life and sense of well-being. I will reject, however, your efforts to include your belief in our body of empirical knowledge, for it is this body that we appeal to in determining public practices and policy, from which we project our plans and goals, on which we act and modify the world. This body of knowledge is public and as such constitutes the foundation of our "public" perception of the world and interaction with the world. Such a foundation must be as free from prejudice, bias, abuse, self-interest as possible to insure the growth of knowledge and promote fair and equitable practices in the world. Making exceptions at the very foundations of knowledge can only quickly encourage including the biases and abuses we are struggling to eliminate.

You might want to consider your own expectations for our body of empirical knowledge and your own response to the question of why can't some knowledge be objective and universal and other knowledge relative.

This examination of our concept of knowledge and the challenge of relativism has brought us through some difficult conceptual terrain. Even though in each of the three positions discussed, relativism appears to simplify many of the complex problems involved in coming to know the world, we have seen how this simplicity obscures rather than clarifies our acquaintance with the world and with ourselves as knowers of the world.

Hence, choosing to pursue a substantial body of knowledge about the world, one characterized by objectivity and universality, means taking on a more difficult and often more frustrating task. The world itself is complex and varied, often easier to ignore than deal with. The choice, then, reflects the extent to which we are willing to confront this world as it is and as we would like it to be. The "rewards" of this confrontation are elusive, not so tangible as the sense of relief that often accompanies an "easy solution" ("Whew, that's over and done with."). Hence though we cannot leave our investigation with that sense of final accomplishment, perhaps there is satisfaction in having achieved some intellectual independence and confidence, in having acquired some of the power that comes with knowledge, and in having arrived at the point where we no longer need to leave solutions in the hands of "the other guy."

Index

150